PHP

Tips and Tricks for Building Modern PHP Apps

Logan Pratt

© Copyright 2020 by Logan Pratt - All rights reserved.

This document is geared towards providing exact and reliable information in regards to the topic and issue covered. The publication is sold with the idea that the publisher is not required to render accounting, officially permitted or otherwise qualified services. If advice is necessary, legal or professional, a practiced individual in the profession should be ordered.

- From a Declaration of Principles which was accepted and approved equally by a Committee of the American Bar Association and a Committee of Publishers and Associations.

In no way is it legal to reproduce, duplicate, or transmit any part of this document in either electronic means or in printed format. Recording of this publication is strictly prohibited, and any storage of this document is not allowed unless with written permission from the publisher. All rights reserved.

The information provided herein is stated to be truthful and consistent, in that any liability, in terms of inattention or otherwise, by any usage or abuse of any policies, processes, or directions contained within is the solitary and utter responsibility of the recipient reader. Under no circumstances will any legal responsibility or blame be held against the publisher for any reparation, damages, or monetary loss due to the information herein, either directly or indirectly.

Respective authors own all copyrights not held by the publisher.

The information herein is offered for informational purposes solely and is universal as so. The presentation of the information is without a contract or any type of guarantee assurance.

The trademarks that are used are without any consent, and the publication of the trademark is without permission or backing by the trademark owner. All trademarks and brands within this book are for clarifying purposes only and are owned by the owners themselves, not affiliated with this document.

TABLE OF CONTENTS

Introduction 1

Chapter One: Installing PHP 9
   Installing a Web Server 9
   Installing PHP 14

Chapter Two: The Basics of PHP 20
   Creating an HTML Page 21
   Analyzing the Script of PHP 22
   PHP Code 26
   PHP Variables 26
   PHP Strings 27
   Joining Strings 28
   Arrays 30

Chapter Three: Creating PHP Scripts 32
   Conditions 32
   Nested if 40
   Switch Statement 41
   Loops 44
   Nesting For Loops 47
   While Loop 54

The Break Statement 62

Chapter Four: Advanced PHP 66

PHP Functions 66

Chapter Five: Object-Oriented Programming 75

Classes 75

Vegetable Class 79

The Constructor Function 80

Destructor 83

PHP Access Modifiers 85

Inheritance 87

Overriding Inheritance 92

Abstract Class 94

Chapter Six: PHP Forms and File Handling 101

PHP File Handling 104

More Examples 106

The Include Factor 110

File Handling 110

Exception Handling 111

Chapter Seven: MySQL Basics 119

MySQL Queries 120

SQL SELECT 120

DISTINCT Statement 123

WHERE Clause 124

AND Statement 127

Combining AND, OR and NOT 132

AND NOT Statements 133

ORDER BY Keyword 135

INSERT INTO Statements 139

Update Table 143

DELETE 152

SELECT TOP 155

COUNT() 159

% Wildcard 160

Charlist Wildcard 163

IN Operator 167

SELECT INTO 171

Chapter Eight: Build Web Applications With PHP 174

Prepend File 174

Classes For Efficiency 177

Code Reuse 178

App Building 181

PHP And HTML 182

User Input 183

Building a PHP CMS 184

Common Errors 192

Chapter Nine: Relevance of PHP in Modern App Development .. 193

Built-in Features 194

Flexibility 195

Popular Databases 195

Chapter Ten: Tips on PHP App Development 198

Laravel 199

PHP Tips 199

v

Conclusion **203**

Resources **206**

Introduction

This book contains proven steps and strategies on how to code in PHP to create web applications. You will learn about the distinct features of PHP in the form of functional codes that you can use in a PHP editor for practice purposes. I have made sure that you'll learn about all the basic and advanced level codes that you will need to create a web app such as a Content Management System (CMS). As MySQL is an integral part of PHP, I have dedicated a chapter on different statements of MySQL, which you can use to operate a database. PHP is hollow without MySQL because each web application requires a database to channelize user information and store it for future usage.

PHP is not too old; we can trace back its origins to 1994 when Rasmus Lerdorf wrote the very first version. It was built, in its initial phases, from the C language as a means of replacing code snippets of Perl that he had been using on the personal homepage that he had. It kept evolving; however, it was 1995 that he released the very first formal as well as the public version of this language. At this point, PHP had been referred to as Personal Homepage Tools. JavaScript was bound to release in 1996 as a client-side language. PHP's release at that time as a server-side language speaks volumes about the tremendous growth in the tools of the Internet that occurred at that time.

In 1998, PHP received its third version that was released by Andi Gutmans and Zeev Suraski. The new version had got its unique name Hypertext Preprocessor. This version awarded PHP sizable popularity. The version 4 of PHP came in 2000 and was referred to as Zend Engine. This version elevated PHP to a level that it had never seen before. It removed certain shortcomings from PHP and made it a fuller language. Version 5 of PHP received its release in 2004 with new features such as an improved version of object-oriented programming and better performance. PHP 7 was released in 2014 and 2015. It further updated PHP for a higher level of web development.

PHP shot to fame when the world got to know that Mark Zuckerberg had used it to create the world-famous application Facebook. When dropped out of Harvard in 2003, Mark adopted this language to create the app, and the Facebook app is still using this language at its backend. Facebook has since developed its own language known as Hack, but it is a version of PHP.

The book contains practical steps to help you understand what happens at the server-side of a web application. It will help you go through the ins and outs of PHP and MySQL that generally go side by side in the creation of a web application. I have divided this chapter into 11 chapters to create ease for the readers. Each chapter of the book deals with a unique topic. I recommend that you download and install a PHP editor or open an online PHP editor for practice purposes while you read the book. You can use the sample codes from the book and understand how they work when they are put in an editor. I hope your journey through the book will be amazing, and you will come out as a knowledgeable person.

The first chapter of the book focuses on the installation of PHP on your computer. It is a complicated process. You should give it a couple of readings to understand how you can do it. The process will not be as much difficult on Linux and Mac OS as it will be on a Windows Operating System. I have explained the topic in a step-by-step order. The first chapter is the installation of the webserver on your operating system, and there are many web servers available in the market. You can choose at will. In the case of this book, I chose to explain the most popular web server of all time that is known as Apache. Apache is a brilliant web server that pairs up with PHP and enhances its performance. When you have downloaded it, you will have to verify Apache. The next step is the installation process. You will find it explained most lucidly and comprehensively. After the installation process completes, you can open Apache and initiate the operations. The final step regarding the webserver is the configuration of Apache. The second half of this chapter focuses on the installation of PHP on your computer system. As it is a server-side language, its installation is a bit tricky and somewhat a tough nut to crack. However, by following the right steps, you can go through it like a breeze. It will be smooth sailing. When you have obtained PHP, you have to verify it. Next comes the task of the configuration of your web server regarding PHP. The chapter ends on explaining the configuration process.

The second chapter of the book focuses on the basics of PHP. I will explain how you should create an HTML page as it is an essential part of PHP. You will be required to embed your PHP code in the HTML document you create. The HTML document will help PHP run the web application. The PHP code will not be visible on the web page when you try to display it. All the code will remain hidden; however, the HTML code will be shown. I will analyze the PHP script for you so that you understand it when you read it in the next sections and write it for practice. This chapter contains valuable information about PHP variables, PHP strings, etc. You will learn how you can use PHP variables for storing information and using it later on.

The third chapter of the book focuses on creating PHP scripts that you would need when you build a web application. The first script, and also one of the most popular in many programming languages, is the conditional statement. A conditional statement can be identified by the keyword 'if.' The if statement comes into play when you have to set more than one condition in the code so that the web application reads through them and acts on them. If the first condition is true, the code doesn't move further and just ends there. If the first condition turns out to be false, the code jumps on to the next condition and runs it. When there are 'else-if' statements, and the first two conditions turn out to be false, the third condition comes into play.

The chapter then moves on to the 'nested if' statements that contain two or more if statements nested inside of one if statement. Next comes PHP loops. They are the most interesting features of PHP. You can insert a loop inside of the code and make tasks easy and somewhat automated. There are three types of loops in PHP. The first that will come under discussion is the *for* loop. I will explain it with an example. Then I will move on to the nested for loops. After that, I will explain what a *while* loop is and how it works. You will see a sufficient amount of examples in these sections, which will create your concepts about these features of PHP. Sometimes, programmers accidentally create infinite loops that make a program run on end. I will explain what an infinite loop is and how it can be created accidentally. The next on the line is the Break statement. This statement is very important to break the infinite loop. If you include it in the code, it will make sure that there are no infinite loops in the code. Coupled with the break statement is the continue statement.

The fourth chapter of the book focuses on the advanced features of PHP language. I will start with PHP functions, which are the most amazing features in the world of PHP. A PHP function makes the server-side coding smart, brief, and fast. All you need is to create a function, and then you can make a function call later on, and all the code that the function contains will start running and doing its job.

You save yourself the hassle of writing the same code over and over again. Everything just fits in the right spot when you choose functions to do the job for you. Functions should be understood in the right manner. There are arguments that you have to pass on to the functions. You can create a function that you can use for the rest of the programming session. I will explain with an example of what PHP arguments are and how you can pass on these arguments to PHP functions. You can add as many arguments to PHP functions as you can. Besides the arguments, you can fill in the functions with a bunch of default values. These default values will come into play if you leave PHP functions empty of arguments. You can fill your function with default values if you are going to use some particular values multiple times throughout a function. In the next section of this chapter, I will shed light on what return values are and what is their significance in the world of coding.

The fifth chapter of the book focuses on the object-oriented programming features of PHP that make the core of a PHP web application. The first on the line in the world of PHP object-oriented programming (OOP) comes classes. PHP classes help you model real-life objects in PHP. You can create a class and then add instances to it to make it work as a real-life object. I will fill in the chapter with the example of a vegetable class. I will define the parameters of the class. Then I will add instances to the same class. The instances for the vegetable class will be vegetables like potato, tomato, and beet. I will give them color, weight, and shape. This kind of program can be effectively used in the creation of an online grocery app. You can fill in the database with the right information and use it at will. If you are creating a car class for a showroom, you can create instances that would fill in a particular object with the name of the model, the year of manufacturing, the color of the car, and its value.

Object oriented programming is the soul of PHP web application development. Next in line is the PHP constructor function. The next section is about the destructor function. In the next section, I will explain what PHP Access Modifiers and how you can use them in creating web applications. The section that contains the topic of inheritance is very important. Inheritance means that you are filling in the PHP classes with child classes. The main class will become the parent class while the other class with the child class. The child class tends to inherit the attributes of the parent class. It will enjoy a distinct status in the code as it will inherit the instances of the parent class and will also keep up its own. This is how you can create child class or small objects inside of the parent class and make the program more complicated and amazing. If you don't want your child class to inherit any of the instances of features of the parent class, you can use the override feature of PHP that will allow you to create a condition in which the child class will not inherit anything from the parent class. The chapter ends on an explanation of the topic of abstract classes.

The sixth chapter of the book focuses on PHP form making and file handling. This chapter is a short one, and it concludes with a brief explanation of exception handling.

The seventh chapter of the book deals with MySQL basics. MySQL and PHP go side by side when you are building a web application. Take the example of Facebook. It is built with PHP on the server-side. Have you ever wondered where the data goes, which you feed on the platform? You upload different types of data such as pictures, videos, text, and numbers, and you can access your data from the past ten years. Facebook holds data of billions of users presently. That's huge. PHP works with MySQL to offer developers a platform to store data in a database. That database is dubbed as MySQL. You can integrate MySQL coding to PHP to channelize your data toward storage. In this chapter, I will give you a glimpse of how you can navigate through the database once you have built a web application. In the first section, I will give you the know-how of SQL queries. I will move on to explaining the SQL SELECT statement as to how you can maneuver the data from the database. I will then proceed toward the explanation of the DISTINCT statement. Then comes the WHERE clause, which you can use to point out the position where you want to implement the code. I will then move on to the explanation of the AND statement, OR statement, and NOT statement. You can update the database and also delete it at will. Generally, a database in MySQL stores the information in the form of tables.

The eighth chapter of the book focuses on building web applications with the help of PHP. I will first explain the Prepend file. Then I will add classes to the code. I will also explain the importance of reusing the code and functions. The first step toward the creation of a web application is to create a PHP file and an HTML file and combining the two. You will learn how to combine the two, as most of the code samples in this book will contain both PHP and HTML codes in a combination. The next section of the chapter focuses on user input because almost all web apps allow users to fill in their information on the website. While you are building a PHP content management system, you will have to create a class and add functions and methods to it.

The ninth chapter of the book focuses on the relevance of PHP in the present day. I will explore the topics of certain built-in features. PHP is gaining ground due to its flexibility and its capacity to pair up with popular databases, and the next section focuses on the benefits of PHP as a developing language. I will explain what a simple API is, what is optimal, what app stability means, and what is maintenance.

The tenth chapter of the book is about the tips on developing app development. You will learn about the most popular PHP app developing platform known as Laravel. You will also get to know about different PHP tips that you can use to make your codes operational and viable.

This book is for everyone who is looking forward to being an expert in the world of website development. You don't have to be a master in the world of coding. However, basic knowledge can be a big plus. Even if you don't have that basic knowledge, the book contains some simple examples which you can understand without any hassle. I recommend that you keep a notebook by your side to note down important tricks that you can use later on while developing your web app. You are allowed to use the codes to practice and hone your skills. I have designed the codes in a way that they have two parts. The first part is what I wrote in the PHP editor, while the second part is what was displayed on the web browser. If you can't see the PHP code in the result, it is because PHP is a server-side language, and the code is always hidden from the eyes of the users.

Chapter One

Installing PHP

This chapter will walk you through the process of the installation of PHP on your computer system. If you are a Linux or Mac user, you will get PHP installed on your computer system from the company. However, sometimes it is not in active mode, but you can do that easily. The real task to install PHP on a Windows operating system. PHP is not pre-installed on Windows computers. When you have installed it, you are required to configure the webserver for processing the PHP code.

Installing a Web Server

The first step of installing PHP is to install a web server on your computer system. You will have to download and install the Apache. If you are using a hosted or company website and you are placing files on another person's server, then you don't have to install the webserver at all. You can use httpd from Apache because it comes mostly free and is one of the highly popular web servers that are used on the Internet. Many other web servers are also available. Microsoft offers Internet Information Services (IIS), and it also includes a development web server with Visual Studio development app. There is another named nginx that you can use to fulfill your development needs. Apache is popular; that's why I will talk about Apache alone in this chapter.

A Windows operating system does not come with Apache pre-installed on it. You have to install it yourself. You can run a test on whether a web server comes installed on your computer system. Open your internet browser and type in http://localhost in the address bar. If the web browser is installed and functional, you will see a web page. There can be an Apache welcome screen that will display some text. If you don't have a web server installed on your system, the page will display the text, 'unable to connect.'

Apache

Apache is a kind of open-source web server that you can download from the internet for free. There are three versions that you can download; Apache 2.0, Apache 2.2, and Apache 2.4. All of these versions are properly supported and timely upgraded. The PHP software tends to run with these versions. You can download Apache from its official website. You can also download the source code for compilation on your operating system. You can use binary files that are already compiled and in a ready-to-run form to be copied to the current location.

Go to http://httpd.apache.org. and scroll down to the version that you want to install on your operating system. The Windows binary file usually comes with an installer that will install, configure, and start Apache. When you click on Win32 Binary MSI Installer, an installer file will be downloaded on your operating system.

Verification of the File

The Apache website offers several methods for the verification of software after you have downloaded it. It comes as a security precaution to make sure that the bad guys don't alter the file. You can use the MD5 method or the PGP method to run the verification of the file. This process is used for the verification of PHP, Apache, and MySQL.

Installation

You can install Apache on any version of Microsoft Windows. To install Apache, you need to make sure that IIS is not already running on the system. Follow the following steps to confirm the installation.

- The file is usually named apache_, which is followed by its version number called win32-x86-no_ssl.msi. Right-click the file and choose Run as Administrator. This will kick off the Installation Wizard. A welcome screen will pop up on your computer screen.

- Now click on Next. The license agreement will be displayed on the screen.

- Now select I Accept the Terms in the License Agreement. Now click on Next. If you opt not to accept the terms, you will not be able to install this software. A screen that carries information about Apache will be displayed.

- Now click Next, and you will see a screen that will display information about Apache.

- You will be requested information that you ought to enter. The first thing you will have to enter is the Domain Name. You ought to enter the domain name like qas.com. If you want to install Apache for testing and you also want to access it from the machine where you have installed it, you can enter localhost.

- The next information is about the Server Name. You ought to enter the server name when you are in the process of installing Apache, such as www.localhost.com. If you want to install Apache for testing and you also want to access it from the machine where you have installed it, you can enter localhost.

- Now it is time to type in the email address where you are looking to forward to receive the email messages about your web server.

- In this step, you have to select whether you want Apache to run as a service, or you need to start Apache when you want to use it manually.

- The installation type screen will be displayed on our computer screen.

- You ought to select an installation type and then click on Next. In most of the cases, you ought to select Complete. Only the advanced users who understand Apache should go for Custom because if you select it, the screens will differ from when you select any other option.

- The next step is to select the directory where you want to install Apache. Afterward, click on Next.

- Until this point, you can go back and change the information that you have entered before you proceed with the installation. When the process of installation is complete, a screen will pop up, which will tell you that the wizard has completed the process of installation.

- Now click Finish to end the installation process and move out of the Installation Wizard.

Starting Apache

When you have installed it, you might want to start Apache. There is a possibility that the Wizard has already started it. However, when you change the configuration settings, you ought to restart Apache before these new settings start working. Anyways, Apache is ready to use. You can locate certain menu items of Apache that you can use for stopping or starting it. You can reach this menu by clicking on Start, entering Programs, and then opening the Apache HTTP Server. Now. Now click Control Apache Server to see what the menu has got for you.

The first option that you can see on the menu is Start. This option will start Apache when it is not running. If you click this item when the Apache is already running, you will see an error message that will say that Apache has been started. The second option in the menu is Stop. You can use it to stop Apache. There is another one that would allow you to Restart if Apache is already running.

You can retrieve plenty of information from Apache by applying a bunch of commands. You can retrieve information by entering the Command Prompt window. To get there, click on Start, then click on Accessories and then enter Command Prompt. Now change to the bin directory where you have installed Apache. If you want to find out which Apache is installed on your computer, you ought to type in the following command in the command prompt window:

```
apache -v
```

If you want to find out the modules that are compiled into Apache, you should type the following command.

```
apache -l
```

You also can start or stop Apache by the following commands.

```
apache -k start
apache -k stop
```

You can see the options that are available by typing the following commands:

```
apache -h
```

Configuration of Apache

When Apache starts, it starts reading information from a particular configuration file. If Apache fails to read the configuration file, it will not start. Apache behaves as per directives. You can change the behavior of Apache by editing the configuration file and then restarting Apache, so it reads the new directives.

If you choose to install PHP, you will need to configure Apache to recognize PHP programs. Apache looks out for certain web page files in a directory and the subdirectories known as Document Root. You can go on to change the location of the Document Root.

Installing PHP

The first step in the installation of PHP is to check whether it is already installed on your operating system or not. You can search your hard drive to look out for any PHP files.

If you are using a Windows operating system, you can use the Find feature to locate PHP in general. Click on Start and then press Find. If you cannot find PHP files on your computer system, PHP is not installed yet on the system. You might have PHP files on your system, but they don't need to be installed on the system. It is also possible that the PHP version that is installed on your computer is not up-to-date.

Obtain PHP

You can download PHP from the internet. Make sure the version you are downloading is the latest. You should only choose to install an older version of PHP if you must maintain or modify the existing code of a website. The code you write with one version of PHP will need modification to be run on another version of PHP.

You can visit www.php.net. to download PHP for all types of operating systems. The source code for the compilation of your operating system is also available for download. Compilation and installation of the source code are easier on Mac and Linux. As already mentioned, you can download binary files to ease off the installation process for Windows.

There is a zip file available on the official website of PHP, which you can download on your system. The zip file of PHP contains the necessary files along with an installer that you can use to install the PHP files. Use the following link to download the zip file for Windows.

    www.php.net/downloads.php.

Now download the zip package, keeping in mind that it should be the most recent version.

You also can obtain a couple of kits that usually install MySQL, PHP, and Apache in one procedure. These kits will simplify the installation process of PHP. However, the software might not include a wide range of features and extensions that you need. XAMPP is a very popular all-in-one installation kit that contains PHP, Apache, and MySQL, and it can be downloaded from www.apachefriends.org/en/xampp.html. Another popular installation kit is WAMPServer. You can get that at www.wampserver.com.

Verification

The PHP website offers methods for the verification of the software after you have downloaded that as a security precaution to make sure that the bad guys have not altered the file. The MD5 method is simpler for the verification process.

If you open the download web page, you can see a long string that is called a signature. It will be displayed below the file that you have downloaded. Let's take a look at an example.

MD5:-6112f6a730c680a4048dbab40e4107b3

The downloaded file must bear the same MD5 signature. PHP runs with many web servers. However, these instructions mainly focus on Internet Information Servers (IIS) and Apache because they power almost 90 percent of the websites that are available on the Internet.

PHP runs on Microsoft Windows smoothly after you have successfully installed it. Remember the zip file that you have just downloaded on your operating system. If you want to install PHP 5 or 6 on your operating system, you have to unzip the file that carries the necessary files for PHP. When you unzip it, it will store the files in the appropriate places. If you don't want to unzip the files, you can use a PHP installer which may be available for the version of Windows you are using. Here is a rundown of the steps involved in the process.

The first step is to extract the files from the .zip file into the directory where you want the PHP to be installed. The location can be anything like c:\php. The zip file is usually named php5.4.5-Win32.zip-. If you give the file a double click, it will open. Now copy them to an appropriate directory or right away extract them. C:\php is the top choice for installation because a lot of configuration files assume that PHP is installed in that location. This will make sure that the default settings are correct.

You ought not to install PHP in a directory with a space in the path like Software Files\PHP. Now you have a directory and many subdirectories that carry the files from the Zip file. Now you must be able to run certain PHP programs. PHP needs files that it cannot locate. If it happens, you will see an error message, saying that it cannot find the .dll extension. You can find the DLL file in the ext subdirectory and then copy it into the major PHP directory.

The second step is the activation of MySQL support. After that, configure the webserver. Finally, it is time to configure the PHP section.

Configuration of Web Server for PHP

Your web server ought to be configured to recognize PHP scripts and run them as well. You cannot have Apache and Internet Information Services (IIS) both running at the same time and by using the same port number. Either you can shut down a web server or direct them to listen on different ports.

You need to edit the Apache configuration file known as httpd.conf before PHP may properly run. PHP also can configure itself to work with Apache. In that case, you will see the LoadModule directive that is present and uncommented. However, if it is not configured, you can use the following steps to do so.

- Open the httpds.comf by reaching into the Apache HTTPD Server folder from the Start menu. Click on Configure Apache Server and then go for Edit Configuration. If you cannot find Edit Configuration on the Start menu, you can find the httpd.conf on the hard drive. You can locate it in the directory where you have installed Apache. Open the file in a text editor like Notepad.

- It is time to activate the PHP module. Look out for the module statement section in the file and then find out the following line:

```
#LoadModule php5_module "c:/php/php5apache2_2.dll."
```

If you want to activate the module, you can remove # from the start of the line. The name of the module may differ, depending on the PHP version and Apache version that you have been using.

- You need to tell Apache which files are PHP programs and which are not. Find out the section that describes AddType. This particular section may contain one or more AddType lines from the other software. The line for PHP is as under:

```
AddType application/x-httpd-php .php
```

Find out the line. If you find it with a pound sign at the start, remove the sign. If there is no such file, you can add it to the list of AddType statements.

- You can start Apache as a service in the later versions of Windows by clicking on Start then Programs, then Apache HTTPD Server, and then Control Apache Server. Now select Start or Restart.

PHP Configuration

PHP uses different settings of a file named php.ini to control its behavior. PHP looks for php.ini when it starts and uses its settings. The default location for php.ini is one of the following unless you change them.

If the php.ini file has not already been installed, you have to do that now. You can look out for a php.ini-dist file that has default settings. The file is included in the PHP distribution. You can copy the file to an appropriate location like the default locations, as mentioned, changing the file to php.ini. If you have a version of PHP installed like PHP 4.3, you can make a backup copy for PHP 5 or 6. Then you take a look at the settings you are presently using.

For the configuration of PHP, open the php.ini file and edit it. Then change the settings that you need to change. If you are using PHP 5 or earlier, you need to turn off magic quotes. Search the following line:

```
magic_quotes-gpc On
```

Change the On to Off.

If you are using PHP 5 or 6 on Windows, you need to activate mysql or mysqli support. You ought to remove the semicolon so that the setting stays active. Also, change 1 to 0. The line looks as follows after the changes:

```
cgi.force_redirect = 0
```

If you are using PHP 5 or later, you need to set the local time zone. Now save php.ini file and then restart your web server.

Chapter Two

The Basics of PHP

PHP is a scripting language that is designed to be used on the web. It has a wide range of features to help you in programming different tasks that are needed to develop several dynamic web applications. This chapter will walk you through the basics of writing PHP scripts, such as the rules that you can apply to different PHP statements. You can take these rules as something similar to general punctuation rules.

The PHP software works just like a web server, which is a software that delivers different web pages to the world. When you type a URL into the address bar of the web browser, you will send a message to the web browser at that URL, telling it to send you an HTML file. The web server will respond by sending the file you had requested. The browser will read the HTML file and then display the web page. The web server will process the file when you click a web page button that would submit a form.

When PHP is installed, the webserver is generally configured to expect file extensions to contain certain PHP language statements. More often the extension is .phtml or .php. When the webserver receives a request for a file that has the designated extension, it will send the HTML statements as they are. When PHP language statements are generally processed, the output is sent by the webserver to the web browser. The PHP statements are not a part of the browser, so the PHP code remains hidden from the user.

Creating an HTML Page

HyperText Markup Language is also a web language. When you open a web page in the web browser such as Google Chrome, Firefox, and Safari, the browser downloads the page, what you see is the HTML page. HTML is just like a document that is much the same as a document you create in a word processor. A program, just like MS Word is required to view and word documents because the MS Processor can only read that format. In the case of HTML, the web browser is a program that reads and displays the documents that are created with HTML.

Unlike a word processor, you cannot create an HTML document with a browser. You have to create HTML documents with the help of an editor. An editor can be a simple one like Notepad or a complex one like Microsoft Visual Studio. We have to understand HTML because we need this language to embed PHP and run it on a browser.

All HTML documents ought to start with <!DOCTYPE html>.

```
<!DOCTYPE html>
<html>
<body>

    <h1>This is an HTML heading</h1>
    <p>This is an example of an HTML
    paragraph.</p>

</body>
</html>
There are three types of headings that you can
use to design HTML headings.
<h1>This is how you can insert a heading 1</h1>
<h2>This is how you can insert heading 2</h2>
<h3>This is how you can insert heading 3</h3>
```

Analyzing the Script of PHP

PHP is well-known as an embedded scripting language when it is used in web pages. It means that you have to use it in an embedded form in HTML code. You have to use HTML tags to write the PHP language. The process is the same as with other HTML documents. You can create and then edit different web pages that contain PHP in the same way you create and edit other HTML pages. The PHP language statements are generally enclosed in the specific PHP tags.

A PHP script may be placed at any position in a word document. The script starts with <?php and it ends with ?>.

```
<html>
    <head>
        <title>This is an example of how a PHP
        script looks like</title>
        </head>
        <body>
<?php
    echo "<h1>We are entering the world of app
development by PHP!</h1>\n";
?>
        </body>
</html>
```

$php main.php

```
<html>
    <head>
        <title>This is an example of how a PHP
        script looks like</title>
        </head>
        <body>
        <h1>We are entering the world of app
        development by PHP!</h1>
        </body>
</html>
```

The browser doesn't show the PHP script in the code. You also can use a shorter version of PHP tags by using just <? and ?>. If you enable short tags, you can be able to spare some time. One problem is that your scripts are not going to run effectively if you move them to another web host where you have not activated PHP short tags.

All PHP statements are processed in between these PHP tags. After the browser has processed the PHP section, it discards it. If there is an output, the PHP section is replaced by the output as you have seen in the above-mentioned example. There can be more than one section to a PHP script. Here is the example.

```
<html>
    <head>
        <title>This is an example of how a PHP script looks like</title>
    </head>
    <body>
    <?php
        echo "<h1>We are entering the world of app development by PHP!</h1>\n";
    ?>
    <?php
        echo "<h2>I am learning app development by PHP!</h1>\n";
    ?>
    </body>
</html>
```

The result of the above script is as under:

$php main.php

```
<html>
    <head>
        <title>This is an example of how a PHP script looks like</title>
    </head>
```

```
        <body>
                <h1>We are entering the world of app
        development by PHP!</h1>
                <h2>I am learning app development by PHP!</h1>
        </body>
</html>
```

If you have been acquainted with Python, you might know that Python is case sensitive. It means that in Python the two words 'class' and 'CLASS' are case sensitive. Let's see how PHP deals with the variety of cases.

```
<html>
        <head>
                <title>This is an example of how a PHP
        script looks like</title>
        </head>
        <body>
                <?php
                        echo "<h1>We are entering the world of
        app development by PHP!</h1>\n";
                ?>
        <?php
                        Echo "<h2>I am learning app
        development by PHP!</h1>\n";
                ?>
        <?php
                        ECHO "<h2>I am learning app
        development by PHP!</h1>\n";
                ?>
        </body>
</html>
```

I have written the same script with three different cases. Let's see the results now.

```
$php main.php
<html>
        <head>
```

```
            <title>This is an example of how a PHP
    script looks like</title>
    </head>
    <body>
            <h1>We are entering the world of app
    development by PHP!</h1>
            <h2>I am learning app development by PHP!</h1>
            <h2>I am learning app development by PHP!</h1>
    </body>
</html>
```

All PHP keywords like if, class and echo are not case-sensitive, however, PHP variables are.

```
<html>
    <head>
            <title>This is an example of how a PHP
    script looks like</title>
    </head>
    <body>
            <?php
            $color = "blue";
            echo "My car is " . $color . "<br>";
            echo "My shoes is " . $COLOR . "<br>";
            echo "My coat is " . $coLOR . "<br>";
            ?>
    </body>
</html>
```

Browser doesn't understand when the case is changed. If you are using an editor to write your scripts, you will see error messages at the bottom of the page.

```
$php main.php
<html>
    <head>
            <title>This is an example of how a PHP
    script looks like</title>
    </head>
```

```
        <body>
                My car is blue<br>My shoes is <br>My coat
        is <br></body>
</html>
```

PHP Notice: Undefined variable: COLOR in /home/cg/root/3268398/main.php on line 9

PHP Notice: Undefined variable: coLOR in /home/cg/root/3268398/main.php on line 10

PHP Code

PHP code ought to be read by humans and the PHP software. When you have written a script for a web application, it will have to be modified and maintained in a year or two. The person who will be tasked with the modification of the code should be able to understand the script. Therefore it must be written in a style that is readable by humans and easier for them to understand.

Each PHP simple statement should be written on a single line and finished with a semicolon. When you write block statements, you should indent each block for a clear read.

PHP Variables

Usually, a PHP variable starts with $ sign and is followed by the name of the variable. The PHP echo is used to display the output on the computer screens. Take a look at the following example to see how the output text is displayed on the computer screens.

```
<html>
        <head>
                <title>Online PHP Script
        Execution</title>
        </head>
        <body>
```

```
        <?php
            $txt = "amazing ";
            echo "PHP is an " . $txt. "language.";
        ?>
    </body>
</html>
```

$php main.php

```
<html>
    <head>
        <title>Online PHP Script
        Execution</title>
    </head>
    <body>
    PHP is an amazing language.</body>
</html>
```

PHP Strings

PHP has character strings that are in the form of a series of characters. These are numbers, letters, and punctuation. When a number is used as a character, it is in the form of a stored character. When you are storing a character in a variable, you are telling PHP where the sting begins and where it ends by using double quotes and single quotes. It will deliver the same result with both types of quotations.

```
<html>
    <head>
        <title>Online PHP Script
        Execution</title>
    </head>
    <body>
        <?php
            $string = "I am invited to dine in at Sally's house.";
            echo $string;
```

```
                ?>
        </body>
</html>
```

$php main.php

```
<html>
        <head>
                <title>Online PHP Script
        Execution</title>
        </head>
        <body>
                I am invited to dine in at Sally's
        house.</body>
</html>
```

Joining Strings

You can join strings through a process known as concatenation by using a dot.

```
<html>
        <head>
                <title>Online PHP Script
        Execution</title>
        </head>
        <body>
                <?php
                        $string1 = "I am invited to dine in at
        Sally's house.";
                        $string2 = " Please join us and have
        fun.";
                        $stringall = $string1.$string2;
                echo $stringall;
                ?>
        </body>
</html>
```

$php main.php

```
<html>
    <head>
        <title>Online PHP Script
    Execution</title>
    </head>
    <body>
        I am invited to dine in at Sally's house.
    Please join us and have fun.</body>
</html>
```

You can add a space between the two strings to display a neat result. PHP offers a feature that is known as heredoc, which you can use to create longer strings that may span over several lines. A heredoc will enable you to tell PHP from where you should start and where you need to end a string. ENDSTRING may include anything that you need to use. You will enclose the piece of text that you want to store in the variable $varname by putting ENDSTRNG at the start and the end. When PHP tends to process the heredoc, it will read the ENDSTRING and will know to begin reading the test into $varname.

```
<html>
    <head>
        <title>Online PHP Script
    Execution</title>
    </head>
    <body>
<?php
    $distance = 50;
    $herevariable = <<<ENDOFTEXT
    You will be intrigued to know that the distance between
    Uganda and Kila Town
    Is $distance kilometers.
    ENDOFTEXT;
    echo $herevariable;
```

```
            ?>
        </body>
</html>
```

$php main.php

```
<html>
    <head>
            <title>Online PHP Script
    Execution</title>
    </head>
    <body>
            You will be intrigued to know that the
    distance between
                Uganda and Kira Town
        Is 50 kilometers.</body>
</html>
```

Arrays

Arrays are considered complex variables. A particular array tends to store a group of values inside of a single variable name. It is quite useful for the storage of related values. You can store the information about a certain flower-like color, variety, and cost. You can handle that information, modify it, and access it.

One of the simplest way to creating an array is to assign a value to a particular variable with square brackets ([ ]) at the end of the name.

```
<html>
    <head>
            <title>Online PHP Script
    Execution</title>
    </head>
    <body>
            <?php
            $countries[1] = "United States";
```

```php
            $countries[2] = "England";
            $countries[3] = "Brazil";
            $countries[4] = "Pakistan";
            $countries[5] = "Egypt";
            echo countries[1];
            ?>
    </body>
</html>
```

Chapter Three

Creating PHP Scripts

PHP scripts generally refer to a series of instructions in a file with an extension that instructs the webserver on looking for PHP sections inside of a file. The extension is usually known as .phtml and .php. Instructions in PHP are labeled as statements that can either be simple or complex. Complex statements tend to execute one or more blocks of statements.

Conditions

Conditions in PHP are expressions that PHP tests or evaluate to verify if the conditions are true and false. PHP conditions are generally used in the form of complex statements to check whether a block that is filled with simple statements can be executed or not. You have to compare different values to set a condition.

The if Statement

The if statement will execute the code if one condition stands true. The first part of the if statement, which you will see in the example, is the 'if' part. If the condition is true, the block of statements is executed. When they are executed, the script will shift to the next instruction by following the conditional statement. If the conditional statement possesses an else-if or else sections, the script will skip over it.

If the condition is false, the block of statements is not executed. The script will skip over to the next instruction that will be an else-if or an else, or any other next instruction after the 'if' conditional statement.

Another keyword in the if statement is known as 'else.' This part is considered optional. Just one 'else' can be integrated into the 'if' statement. It is not meant to test any condition. However, it is aimed at executing a block of statements. The script tends to enter the else section when the 'if' section and the 'else-if' sections are not true. Let's try an if else statement.

```html
<html>
    <head>
        <title>This is PHP</title>
    </head>
    <body>
        <?php
        $t = date("H");

        if ($t < "15") {
           echo "Welcome! I wish you a good day!";
        } else {
           echo "Good night! I have to go now!";
        }
        ?>
    </body>
</html>
```

$php main.php

```html
<html>
    <head>
        <title>This is PHP</title>
    </head>
    <body>
```

Welcome! I wish you a good day!</body>
</html>

Here is a block of code that contains the if-else statements in their entirety.

```
<html>
    <head>
        <title>This is PHP</title>
    </head>
    <body>
        <?php
        $thescore = 100;
        if ($thescore > 95 )
            {
             $thegrade = "A";
             $themessage = "This is
            Excellent!";
            }
        else-if ($thescore <= 95 and $thescore > 85 )
            {
             $thegrade = "B";
             $themessage = "This is Very
            Good!";
            }
        else-if ($thescore <= 85 and $thescore > 75 )
            {
             $thegrade = "C";
             $themessage = "This is Okay. Not
            as much good as it should have";
            }
        else-if ($thescore <= 75 and $thescore > 65 )
            {
             $thegrade = "D";
             $themessage = "Not good. In fact
            really bad!";
```

```
                }
            else
                {
                 $thegrade = "F";
                 $themessage = "You are doomed!";
                }
            echo $themessage."\n";
            echo "Your grade is $thegrade\n";
            ?>
        </body>
</html>
```

$php main.php

```
<html>
    <head>
        <title>This is PHP</title>
    </head>
    <body>
        This is Excellent!
        Your grade is A
    </body>
</html>
```

Now I will change the score value and let the second block of code work. Here is the example.

```
<html>
    <head>
        <title>This is PHP</title>
    </head>
    <body>
        <?php
        $thescore = 90;
        if ($thescore > 95 )
            {
                $thegrade = "n";
```

```
            $themessage = "This is
            Excellent!";
            }
        else-if ($thescore <= 95 and $thescore >
        85 )
            {
             $thegrade = "B";
             $themessage = "This is Very
            Good!";
            }
        else-if ($thescore <= 85 and $thescore >
        75 )
            {
             $thegrade = "C";
             $themessage = "This is Okay. Not
            as much good as it should have";
            }
        else-if ($thescore <= 75 and $thescore >
        65 )
            {
             $thegrade = "D";
             $themessage = "Not good. In fact
            really bad!";
            }
        else
            {
             $thegrade = "F";
             $themessage = "You are doomed!";
            }
        echo $themessage."\n";
        echo "Your grade is $thegrade\n";
        ?>
    </body>
</html>
```

$php main.php

```
<html>
    <head>
        <title>This is PHP</title>
    </head>
    <body>
        This is Very Good!
        Your grade is B
    </body>
</html>
```

In the following example, I will enter the value that is less than 85 so that the third else-if statement can be deployed to work. The browser will ignore the 'if statement and the first else-if statement.

```
<html>
    <head>
        <title>This is PHP</title>
    </head>
    <body>
        <?php
        $thescore = 80;
        if ($thescore > 95 )
            {
              $thegrade = "n";
              $themessage = "This is
              Excellent!";
            }
        else-if ($thescore <= 95 and $thescore >
        85 )
            {
              $thegrade = "B";
              $themessage - "This is Very
              Good!";
            }
        else-if ($thescore <= 85 and $thescore >
        75 )
            {
```

```
                    $thegrade = "C";
                    $themessage = "This is Okay. Not
                as much good as it should have";
                    }
            else-if ($thescore <= 75 and $thescore >
            65 )
                    {
                    $thegrade = "D";
                    $themessage = "Not good. In fact
                    really bad!";
                    }
            else
                    {
                    $thegrade = "F";
                    $themessage = "You are doomed!";
                    }
            echo $themessage."\n";
            echo "Your grade is $thegrade\n";
            ?>
        </body>
</html>
```

$php main.php

```
<html>
    <head>
        <title>This is PHP</title>
    </head>
    <body>
        This is Okay. Not as much good as it
        should have
        Your grade is C
    </body>
</html>
```

Let's check out the last option.

```
<html>
    <head>
        <title>This is PHP</title>
    </head>
    <body>
        <?php
        $thescore = 60;
        if ($thescore > 95 )
            {
              $thegrade = "n";
              $themessage = "This is
            Excellent!";
            }
        else-if ($thescore <= 95 and $thescore >
        85 )
            {
              $thegrade = "B";
              $themessage = "This is Very
            Good!";
            }
        else-if ($thescore <= 85 and $thescore >
        75 )
            {
              $thegrade = "C";
              $themessage = "This is Okay. Not
            as much good as it should have";
            }
        else-if ($thescore <= 75 and $thescore >
        65 )
            {
              $thegrade = "D";
              $themessage = "Not good. In fact
            really bad!";
            }
        else
            {
              $thegrade = "F";
```

```
                        $themessage = "You are doomed!";
                    }
                echo $themessage."\n";
                echo "Your grade is $thegrade\n";
                ?>
        </body>
</html>
```

$php main.php

```
<html>
        <head>
                <title>This is PHP</title>
        </head>
        <body>
                You are doomed!
                Your grade is F
        </body>
</html>
```

Nested if

You can put and if conditional statement inside of another if conditional statement. This process is known as nesting. Suppose you have to contact your customers living in Minnesota. You are planning to send emails to their IDs and then send written letters to those who don't keep email addresses. You can identify the groups of customers by the following method.

```
if ( $thecustState == "ID" )
    {
            if ( $theEmailAdd = "" )
        {
            $thecontactMethod = "letter";
        }
  else
```

```
        {
            $thecontactMethod = "contact through
    email";
        }
}
else
        {
            $thecontactMethod = "there is none needed";
}
```

Switch Statement

The switch statement is aimed at testing the value of $variablename. The script moves on to the case section and executes the statements until a break statement comes or the switch statement reaches it end. You are free to use as many sections as you want to. If you opt to use a default section, you can put the default at the end.

```
<html>
    <head>
        <title>This is PHP</title>
    </head>
    <body>
        <?php
        $favoritecolor = "green";

        switch ($favoritecolor) {
          case "green":
            echo "My favorite color is green!";
            break;
          case "purple":
            echo "My favorite color is purple!";
            break;
          case "violet":
            echo "My favorite color is violet!";
            break;
          default:
            echo "My favorite color is none of
        those stated!";
```

```
            }
        ?>
    </body>
</html>
```

$php main.php

```
<html>
    <head>
        <title>This is PHP</title>
    </head>
    <body>
        My favorite color is green!</body>
</html>
```

Let's change the name of the color in the code and see the results.

```
<html>
    <head>
        <title>This is PHP</title>
    </head>
    <body>
        <?php
        $favoritecolor = "violet";

        switch ($favoritecolor) {
          case "green":
            echo "My favorite color is green!";
            break;
          case "purple":
            echo "My favorite color is purple!";
            break;
          case "violet":
            echo "My favorite color is violet!";
            break;
          default:
```

```
            echo "My favorite color is none of
            those stated!";
            }
            ?>
    </body>
</html>
```

$php main.php

```
<html>
    <head>
        <title>This is PHP</title>
    </head>
    <body>
            My favorite color is violet!</body>
</html>
```

In the third code snippet, I will choose a color that is not in the case statements. Let's see what the result is.

```
<html>
    <head>
        <title>This is PHP</title>
    </head>
    <body>
            <?php
            $favoritecolor = "yellow";

            switch ($favoritecolor) {
              case "green":
                echo "My favorite color is green!";
                break;
              case "purple":
                echo "My favorite color is purple!";
                break;
              case "violet":
                echo "My favorite color is violet!";
```

```
            break;
        default:
            echo "My favorite color is none of
    those stated!";
        }
        ?>
    </body>
</html>
```

$php main.php

```
<html>
    <head>
        <title>This is PHP</title>
    </head>
    <body>
            My favorite color is none of those
    stated!</body>
</html>
```

Loops

You are used, in general, in scripts when you have to set up a block of different statements that would repeat themselves. The PHP loop can repeat itself for an unlimited period. You can create a loop that contains the names of the countries of the world. The loop would echo the names of the countries until you set a condition which it would meet and stop. A loop can give you the names of certain files in a directory until the directory stands empty.

Loop Types

The first type is the *for loop*. It sets up a counter that would repeat the block of statement that you fill it with until the counter reaches a particular number.

The second type is the *while loop*. It sets up a condition that would check the condition and see if it is true and then repeat a certain block of statements until the condition stands false.

The third type is the do…while loop that also sets up a condition. After that it executes a block of statements until the condition stands false. There is an init counter that will initialize the counter value of the loop. Then there is a test counter that is evaluated for each iteration of the loop. If the evaluation is TRUE, the loop goes on. Otherwise, it ends there. The increment counter will increase the counter value of the loop.

```
<html>
    <head>
        <title>This is PHP</title>
    </head>
    <body>
        <?php
        for ($y = 0; $y <= 20; $y++) {
          echo "The requisite number is: $y
        <br>";
        }
        ?>
    </body>
</html>

        $php main.php
        <html>
        <head>
        <title>This is PHP</title>
    </head>
<body>
        The requisite number is: 0 /n<br>The
        requisite number is: 1 /n<br>The
        requisite number is: 2 /n<br>The
        requisite number is: 3 /n<br>The
        requisite number is: 4 /n<br>The
        requisite number is: 5 /n<br>The
```

```
requisite number is: 6 /n<br>The
requisite number is: 7 /n<br>The
requisite number is: 8 /n<br>The
requisite number is: 9 /n<br>The
requisite number is: 10 /n<br>The
requisite number is: 11 /n<br>The
requisite number is: 12 /n<br>The
requisite number is: 13 /n<br>The
requisite number is: 14 /n<br>The
requisite number is: 15 /n<br>The
requisite number is: 16 /n<br>The
requisite number is: 17 /n<br>The
requisite number is: 18 /n<br>The
requisite number is: 19 /n<br>The
requisite number is: 20 /n<br></body>
```
</html>

$y = 0; has initialized the counter of the loop, setting the starting value at 0. In the next example, I will instruct the loop to count by the adding 20 in each loop cycle.

```
<html>
    <head>
        <title>This is PHP</title>
    </head>
    <body>
        <?php
            for ($y = 0; $y <= 200; $y+=20) {
                echo "The requisite number is: $y
                <br>";
            }
        ?>
    </body>
</html>
```

$php main.php

```
<html>
      <head>
            <title>This is PHP</title>
      </head>
<body>
            The requisite number is: 0 <br>The
            requisite number is: 20 <br>The requisite
            number is: 40 <br>The requisite number
            is: 60 <br>The requisite number is: 80
            <br>The requisite number is: 100 <br>The
            requisite number is: 120 <br>The
            requisite number is: 140 <br>The
            requisite number is: 160 <br>The
            requisite number is: 180 <br>The
            requisite number is: 200 <br></body>
</html>
```

Nesting For Loops

You can nest one for loop inside of another for loop. We can create the table of 12 through multiplication from 1 to 12 by using two for loops which will work together.

```
<html>
      <head>
            <title>This is PHP</title>
      </head>
      <body>
            <?php
            for($a=1;$a<=12;$a++)
            {
              echo "\nMultiply by $a \n";
              for($b=1;$b<=12;$b++)
                  {
                      $result = $a * $b;
```

```
                    echo "$a x $b = $result\n";
                }
        }
        ?>
    </body>
</html>
```

$php main.php

```
<html>
    <head>
        <title>This is PHP</title>
    </head>
    <body>
```

Multiply by 1

```
                1 x 1 = 1
                1 x 2 = 2
                1 x 3 = 3
                1 x 4 = 4
                1 x 5 = 5
                1 x 6 = 6
                1 x 7 = 7
                1 x 8 = 8
                1 x 9 = 9
                1 x 10 = 10
                1 x 11 = 11
                1 x 12 = 12
```

Multiply by 2

```
                2 x 1 = 2
                2 x 2 = 4
                2 x 3 = 6
                2 x 4 = 8
                2 x 5 = 10
```

2 x 6 = 12
2 x 7 = 14
2 x 8 = 16
2 x 9 = 18
2 x 10 = 20
2 x 11 = 22
2 x 12 = 24

Multiply by 3

3 x 1 = 3
3 x 2 = 6
3 x 3 = 9
3 x 4 = 12
3 x 5 = 15
3 x 6 = 18
3 x 7 = 21
3 x 8 = 24
3 x 9 = 27
3 x 10 = 30
3 x 11 = 33
3 x 12 = 36

Multiply by 4

4 x 1 = 4
4 x 2 = 8
4 x 3 = 12
4 x 4 = 16
4 x 5 = 20
4 x 6 = 24
4 x 7 = 28
4 x 8 = 32
4 x 9 = 36
4 x 10 = 40
4 x 11 = 44
4 x 12 = 48

Multiply by 5

5 x 1 = 5
5 x 2 = 10
5 x 3 = 15
5 x 4 = 20
5 x 5 = 25
5 x 6 = 30
5 x 7 = 35
5 x 8 = 40
5 x 9 = 45
5 x 10 = 50
5 x 11 = 55
5 x 12 = 60

Multiply by 6

6 x 1 = 6
6 x 2 = 12
6 x 3 = 18
6 x 4 = 24
6 x 5 = 30
6 x 6 = 36
6 x 7 = 42
6 x 8 = 48
6 x 9 = 54
6 x 10 = 60
6 x 11 = 66
6 x 12 = 72

Multiply by 7

7 x 1 = 7
7 x 2 = 14
7 x 3 = 21
7 x 4 = 28
7 x 5 = 35
7 x 6 = 42
7 x 7 = 49

```
7 x 8 = 56
7 x 9 = 63
7 x 10 = 70
7 x 11 = 77
7 x 12 = 84
```

Multiply by 8

```
8 x 1 = 8
8 x 2 = 16
8 x 3 = 24
8 x 4 = 32
8 x 5 = 40
8 x 6 = 48
8 x 7 = 56
8 x 8 = 64
8 x 9 = 72
8 x 10 = 80
8 x 11 = 88
8 x 12 = 96
```

Multiply by 9

```
9 x 1 = 9
9 x 2 = 18
9 x 3 = 27
9 x 4 = 36
9 x 5 = 45
9 x 6 = 54
9 x 7 = 63
9 x 8 = 72
9 x 9 = 81
9 x 10 = 90
9 x 11 = 99
9 x 12 = 108
```

Multiply by 10

10 x 1 = 10
10 x 2 = 20
10 x 3 = 30
10 x 4 = 40
10 x 5 = 50
10 x 6 = 60
10 x 7 = 70
10 x 8 = 80
10 x 9 = 90
10 x 10 = 100
10 x 11 = 110
10 x 12 = 120

Multiply by 11

11 x 1 = 11
11 x 2 = 22
11 x 3 = 33
11 x 4 = 44
11 x 5 = 55
11 x 6 = 66
11 x 7 = 77
11 x 8 = 88
11 x 9 = 99
11 x 10 = 110
11 x 11 = 121
11 x 12 = 132

Multiply by 12

12 x 1 = 12
12 x 2 = 24
12 x 3 = 36
12 x 4 = 48
12 x 5 = 60
12 x 6 = 72
12 x 7 = 84

```
                12 x 8 = 96
                12 x 9 = 108
                12 x 10 = 120
                12 x 11 = 132
                12 x 12 = 144
        </body>
</html>
```

Advanced For Loop

The structure of a for loop is flexible, and it allows you to build loops to achieve different purposes. The basic for loop, which is discussed in this section, has one statement at the start, a conditional statement in the middle, and an incremental section at the end. The general format of the loop allows multiple statements in each section.

The statement, which comes at the start, executes just once. They set a starting value that you ought to execute before the loop initiates a run. The conditional statements are then tested for all iterations of the loop. Then come the ending statements that execute once at the end of the loop. They increment the values that you are looking forward to execute at the end of the 'for' loop.

```
<html>
        <head>
                <title>This is PHP</title>
        </head>
        <body>
                <?php
                $t = 0;
                for ($a=0,$b=1;$t<=15;$a++,$b++)
                        {
                        $t = $a + $b;
                        echo "$t<br />";
                        }
                ?>
        </body>
</html>
```

$php main.php

```
<html>
    <head>
        <title>This is PHP</title>
    </head>
    <body>
        1<br />3<br />5<br />7<br />9<br />11<br
        />13<br />15<br />17<br /></body>
</html>
```

While Loop

A while loop repeats itself until a condition stands true. The loop works in the following manner.

- At the start, you can set up a condition.

- The condition is then tested at the top of each single loops.

- If the certain condition stands true, the loop will repeat itself. If the condition is false, the loop will stop.

Here is a while loop that will neatly display the names of vegetables.

```
<html>
    <head>
        <title>This is PHP</title>
    </head>
    <body>
        <?php
        $vegetables = array ( "pumpkin",
        "carrot", "radish", "beet", "tomato",
        "potato");
        $testvariable = "no";
        $k = 0;
        while ( $testvariable != "yes" )
```

```
            {
            if ($vegetables[$k] == "tomato" )
                {
                $testvariable = "yes";
                echo "Now we have a tomato.\n";
                }
            else
                {
                echo "$vegetables[$k] is not a
                tomato\n";
                }
            $k++;
            }
            ?>
    </body>
</html>
```

$php main.php

```
<html>
    <head>
        <title>This is PHP</title>
    </head>
    <body>
            pumpkin is not a tomato
            carrot is not a tomato
            radish is not a tomato
            beet is not a tomato
            Now we have a tomato.
    </body>
</html>
```

In the following example, I will change the vegetable and see how the loop works.

```
<html>
    <head>
```

```
            <title>This is PHP</title>
        </head>
        <body>
            <?php
            $vegetables = array ( "pumpkin",
            "carrot", "radish", "beet", "tomato",
            "potato");
            $testvariable = "no";
            $k = 0;
            while ( $testvariable != "yes" )
            {
              if ($vegetables[$k] == "potato" )
                    {
                    $testvariable = "yes";
                    echo "Now we have a potato.\n";
                    }
              else
                    {
                    echo "$vegetables[$k] is not a
                    potato\n";
                    }
              $k++;
            }
            ?>
        </body>
</html>
```

$php main.php

```
<html>
    <head>
        <title>This is PHP</title>
    </head>
    <body>
            pumpkin is not a potato
            carrot is not a potato
            radish is not a potato
```

56

```
                beet is not a potato
                tomato is not a potato
                Now we have a potato.
        </body>
</html>
```

The do...while Loop

The do...while loop tends to loop through a certain block of code once at the start and then it keeps on repeating itself as long as the condition stands true. It will execute the code once, check the condition and then repeat the loop as long as the condition is true. Many programmers put the do...while loop and the while loop in the same place, however, a do...while loop tests a set of conditions at the bottom of the loops. If the condition stands true, the loop starts repeating itself. If the condition is false, the do...while loop ceases to work.

```
<html>
        <head>
                <title>This is PHP</title>
        </head>
        <body>
                <?php
                $vegetables = array ( "pumpkin",
                "carrot", "radish", "beet", "tomato",
                "potato");
                $testvariable = "no";
                $k = 0;
                do
                {
                 if ($vegetables[$k] == "beet" )
                        {
                        $testvariable = "yes";
                        echo "Now we have a beet.\n";
                        }
                        else
                        {
```

```
            echo "$vegetables[$k] is not a
            potato\n";
             }
             $k++;
            } while ($testvariable != "yes");
            ?>
        </body>
</html>
```

$php main.php

```
<html>
    <head>
        <title>This is PHP</title>
    </head>
    <body>
            pumpkin is not a potato
            carrot is not a potato
            radish is not a potato
            Now we have a beet.
    </body>
</html>
```

In the next code snippet, I will change the vegetable from beet to potato. Let's take a look at the result of the code.

```
<html>
    <head>
        <title>This is PHP</title>
    </head>
    <body>
            <?php
            $vegetables = array ( "pumpkin",
            "carrot", "radish", "beet", "tomato",
            "potato");
            $testvariable = "no";
            $k = 0;
```

```php
            do
            {
             if ($vegetables[$k] == "potato" )
                    {
                    $testvariable = "yes";
                    echo "Now we have a potato.\n";
                    }
                else
                    {
                    echo "$vegetables[$k] is not a
                    potato\n";
                    }
                $k++;
            } while ($testvariable != "yes");
            ?>
    </body>
</html>
```

$php main.php

```
<html>
    <head>
        <title>This is PHP</title>
    </head>
    <body>
            pumpkin is not a potato
            carrot is not a potato
            radish is not a potato
            beet is not a potato
            tomato is not a potato
            Now we have a potato.
    </body>
</html>
```

If you take a closer look at the above-mentioned code examples, you will realize the fact that the output of the while loop and the do...while loop are the same. What makes the two loops different is that in the while loop, the condition is checked at the top of the code and in the do...while loop, the condition is generally checked at the bottom of the code. If we set the value of the testvariable at 'yes,' the condition stands false right from the start, which means that the code block never runs. See the following code example.

```
<html>
    <head>
        <title>This is PHP</title>
    </head>
    <body>
        <?php
        $vegetables = array ( "pumpkin",
        "carrot", "radish", "beet", "tomato",
        "potato");
        $testvariable = "yes";
        $k = 0;
        do
        {
          if ($vegetables[$k] == "potato" )
                {
                $testvariable = "yes";
                echo "Now we have a potato.\n";
                }
            else
                {
                echo "$vegetables[$k] is not a
                potato\n";
                }
            $k++;
        } while ($testvariable != "yes");
        ?>
    </body>
</html>
```

$php main.php

```
<html>
    <head>
        <title>This is PHP</title>
    </head>
    <body>
        pumpkin is not a potato
    </body>
</html>
```

Infinite Loops

You can set up loops that will run on end, never stopping anywhere. We name them infinite loops. They will go on repeating forever. In most cases, these loops are created accidentally. Consider them a mistake in the code. A slight change in the code may set up a while loop that will be an infinite loop.

```
<html>
    <head>
        <title>This is PHP</title>
    </head>
    <body>
        <?php
        $vegetables = array ( "pumpkin",
        "carrot", "radish", "beet", "tomato",
        "potato");
        $testvariable = "no";
        while ( $testvariable != "yes" )
        {
         $k = 0;
         if ($vegetables[$k] == "potato" )
                {
                $testvariable = "yes";
                echo "Now we have a potato.\n";
                }
            else
                {
```

61

```
                    echo "$vegetables[$k] is not a
                        potato\n";
                        }
            $k++;
        }
        ?>
    </body>
</html>
```

The loop will keep running forever. Just a change in position can create an infinite loop.

The Break Statement

Sometimes you desire to break out of the loop. There are two statements to achieve this purpose. The break will help you break out of the loop at whichever point you want and continue the statement after the loop. The continue statement, which can be paired up with the break statement, will skip the code to the end where a particular condition is repeatedly tested. If its test positive, the script will continue at the top.

These statements are used in conditional statements. The break statement is more often used in switch statements.

```
<html>
    <head>
        <title>This is PHP</title>
    </head>
    <body>
        <?php
        $thecounter = 0;
        while ( $thecounter < 15 )
        {
          $thecounter++;
          If ( $thecounter == 13 )
              {
                echo "break\n";
```

```
                    break;
                }
            echo "This is the last line in the loop:
            counter=$thecounter\n";
            }
            echo "This is the line after loop\n\n";
            ?>
        </body>
</html>
```

$php main.php

```
<html>
        <head>
                <title>This is PHP</title>
        </head>
        <body>
                This is the last line in the loop:
                counter=1
                This is the last line in the loop:
                counter=2
                This is the last line in the loop:
                counter=3
                This is the last line in the loop:
                counter=4
                This is the last line in the loop:
                counter=5
                This is the last line in the loop:
                counter=6
                This is the last line in the loop:
                counter=7
                This is the last line in the loop:
                counter=8
                This is the last line in the loop:
                counter=9
                This is the last line in the loop:
                counter=10
                This is the last line in the loop:
                counter=11
```

63

```
                    This is the last line in the loop:
                    counter=12
                    break
                    This is the line after loop

        </body>
</html>
```

The loop broke at one point and then the rest of the code continued.

```
<html>
    <head>
        <title>This is PHP</title>
    </head>
    <body>
        <?php
        $thecounter = 0;
        while ( $thecounter < 12 )
        {
         $thecounter++;
         If ( $thecounter == 10 )
              {
               echo "this will continue the
              loop\n";
               continue;
              }
          echo "This is the last line in the loop:
          counter=$thecounter\n";
        }
        echo "This is the line after loop\n\n";
        ?>
    </body>
</html>
```

$php main.php

```
<html>
	<head>
		<title>This is PHP</title>
</head>
	<body>
		This is the last line in the loop: counter=1
		This is the last line in the loop: counter=2
		This is the last line in the loop: counter=3
		This is the last line in the loop: counter=4
		This is the last line in the loop: counter=5
		This is the last line in the loop: counter=6
		This is the last line in the loop: counter=7
		This is the last line in the loop: counter=8
		This is the last line in the loop: counter=9
		this will continue the loop
		This is the last line in the loop: counter=11
		This is the last line in the loop: counter=12
		This is the line after loop

	</body>
</html>
```

If you are worried about infinite loops, you can insert a break statement in the code.

Chapter Four

Advanced PHP

More often, applications have to perform several tasks at multiple points in the script. PHP functions let you reuse the same code in several locations as per your need. A function generally is a group of statements in PHP that are designed as such to perform a particular task.

PHP Functions

In the following example, I will create a PHP function example. Curly braces in a function mark the start and the end of the function. When you need to call the function, you can simply write its name.

```
<html>
    <head>
        <title>This is PHP function</title>
    </head>
    <body>
        <?php
        function greetings() {
          echo "Good morning! Hope you are fine!";
        }

        greetings(); // This is how you can call the function
        ?>
    </body>
</html>
```

$php main.php

```
<html>
      <head>
            <title>This is PHP function</title>
      </head>
      <body>
            Good morning! Hope you are fine!</body>
</html>
```

Take a look at another example.

```
<html>
      <head>
            <title>This is PHP function</title>
      </head>
      <body>
            <?php

            function format_your_name()
                  {
                   global $formatted_name;
                   $your_first_name = "Chris";
                   $your_last_name = "Angel";
                   $formatted_name = $your_last_name.
                   "," .$your_first_name;
                   }
            format_your_name();
            echo "$formatted_name";
            ?>
      </body>
</html>
```


$php main.php

```
<html>
      <head>
```

```
            <title>This is PHP function</title>
        </head>
        <body>
            Angel,Chris</body>
</html>
```

If you have to create the variables outside of the function, you can't do that unless you insert a global variable in the code. See the example in which the variables are placed outside of the script.

Arguments

You can pass on information to functions with the help of arguments. An argument acts just like a variable. They are specified after the name of the function inside of the parenthesis. You can add as many variables to a function as you want to.

```
<html>
    <head>
        <title>This is PHP function</title>
    </head>
    <body>
        <?php
        function greetings($name) {
           echo "$name, welcome to the bachelor's club.<br>";
        }

            greetings("John");
            greetings("Sylvia");
            greetings("Sim");
            greetings("Kai Jim");
            greetings("Ben");
            ?>
    </body>
</html>
```

$php main.php

```
<html>
    <head>
        <title>This is PHP function</title>
    </head>
<body>
```

John, welcome to the bachelor's club.
Sylvia, welcome to the bachelor's club.
Sim, welcome to the bachelor's club.
Kai Jim, welcome to the bachelor's club.
Ben, welcome to the bachelor's club.
</body>

```
</html>
```

You also can scale up the script by adding more arguments. In the next example, I will add two arguments in the script.

```
<html>
    <head>
        <title>This is PHP function</title>
    </head>
    <body>
        <?php
        function greetings($name, $year) {
           echo "$name, welcome to the adult's club. I suppose you are born in $year <br>";
        }

        greetings("John" , "1999");
        greetings("Sylvia" , "1988");
        greetings("Sim" , "1995");
        greetings("Kai Jim" , "2001");
        greetings("Ben" , "2002");
        ?>
    </body>
</html>
```

$php main.php

```
<html>
    <head>
        <title>This is PHP function</title>
    </head>
<body>
```

John, welcome to the adult's club. I suppose you are born in 1999
Sylvia, welcome to the adult's club. I suppose you are born in 1988
Sim, welcome to the adult's club. I suppose you are born in 1995
Kai Jim, welcome to the adult's club. I suppose you are born in 2001
Ben, welcome to the adult's club. I suppose you are born in 2002
</body>

```
</html>
```

Default Values

You can use default values for arguments so if you leave the argument section empty, you will still be able to call the function.

```
<html>
    <head>
        <title>This is PHP function</title>
    </head>
    <body>
        <?php
        function greetings($name = "Tom", $year = 1996) {
          echo "$name, welcome to the adult's club. I suppose you are born in $year <br>";
        }

        greetings("John" , "1999");
        greetings("Sylvia" , "1988");
        greetings();
        greetings("Kai Jim" , "2001");
```

```
            greetings();
            ?>
       </body>
</html>
```

$php main.php

```
<html>
     <head>
          <title>This is PHP function</title>
     </head>
<body>
```

John, welcome to the adult's club. I suppose you are born in 1999
Sylvia, welcome to the adult's club. I suppose you are born in 1988
Tom, welcome to the adult's club. I suppose you are born in 1996
Kai Jim, welcome to the adult's club. I suppose you are born in 2001
Tom, welcome to the adult's club. I suppose you are born in 1996
</body>

```
     </html>
```

Return Values

If you want a function to return values, you have to insert in the code the 'return' statement.

```
<html>
     <head>
          <title>This is PHP function</title>
     </head>
     <body>
          <?php
          function sumup(int $a, int $b) {
            $c = $a + $b;
            return $c;
          }
```

```
            echo "45 + 10 = " . sumup(45, 10) .
            "<br>";
            echo "57 + 13 = " . sumup(57, 13) .
            "<br>";
            echo "29 + 41 = " . sumup(29, 41);
            ?>
    </body>
</html>
```

$php main.php

```
<html>
    <head>
            <title>This is PHP function</title>
    </head>
    <body>
            45 + 10 = 55<br>57 + 13 = 70<br>29 + 41 =
    70</body>
</html>
```

Insert Right Arguments

Functions are sensitive in regard to the number of values that you have to pass on to it. If you don't send enough of them, the function will detect the missing values. You will see a warning message when you execute the code.

```
<html>
    <head>
            <title>This is PHP function</title>
    </head>
    <body>
            <?php
            function greetings($name , $year) {
```

```
            echo "$name, welcome to the adult's
            club. I suppose you are born in $year
            <br>";
            }

            greetings("John" , 1999);
            greetings( "Sim", 1988);
            greetings("Drake" , 2000);
            greetings("Kai Jim" , 2001);
            greetings( 2002);
            ?>
     </body>
</html>
```

$php main.php

```
<html>
     <head>
          <title>This is PHP function</title>
     </head>
<body>
```

John, welcome to the adult's club. I suppose you are born in 1999
Sim, welcome to the adult's club. I suppose you are born in 1988
Drake, welcome to the adult's club. I suppose you are born in 2000
Kai Jim, welcome to the adult's club. I suppose you are born in 2001

PHP Fatal error: Uncaught ArgumentCountError: Too few arguments to function greetings(), 1 passed in /home/cg/root/1842013/main.php on line 15 and exactly 2 expected in /home/cg/root/1842013/main.php:7

Stack trace:

```
#0 /home/cg/root/1842013/main.php(15):
greetings(2002)
#1 {main}
  thrown in /home/cg/root/1842013/main.php on
line 7
```

You can see the error that the missing argument has triggered.

Chapter Five

Object-Oriented Programming

Object-oriented programming (OOP) is a particular approach to programming that spans around classes and objects. It is one of the most popular uses of PHP nowadays. PHP5 was released as an improved version of object-oriented programming. It had more speed and improved features. Object-oriented programming, OOP in its short form, is not about using a different syntax, it is about giving you a different approach to analyze problems and carve out their solutions. In OOP, the script is seen as a bunch of different objects, which represent the elements of the problem the script has to solve. If the script is about a used-car lot, the objects can be customers and cars. OOP has brought to light new concepts and terminology.

Classes

One of the basic elements of object-oriented programming is objects. You can take them as physical objects in the form of codes. A PHP object can be a car, a cat, or a dog. You can give them certain properties, known as attributes in the world of programming. For example, a cat can have attributes like sitting down, rolling on the ground, etc. A car can have attributes like color, model, and company name.

A class in PHP code serves as the template that is used for the creation of an object. The class generally defines the attributes, the properties of a particular object. It will also define a wide range of things that the object does like its responsibilities. You write a class that would define a car with an engine and four wheels. The class lists the things that a car can do, like it can move forward and park as well. You also can write a statement like the one as under:

```html
<html>
    <head>
        <title>This is PHP function</title>
    </head>
    <body>
        <?php
        class Vegetables {
          // these are the Properties
          public $vname;
          public $vcolor;

          // these are the Methods
          function set_name($vname) {
            $this->vname = $vname;
          }
          function get_name() {
            return $this->vname;
          }
        }
        ?>
    </body>
</html>
```

In classes, variables are labeled as properties while functions are dubbed as methods. Classes are nothing without objects. You can have the liberty to create a wide range of objects from a single class. Each object contains certain properties and methods that are defined in that class, however, they have varying property values. The *new* keyword is used to create objects of a class. Then there are instances of the class Vegetables.

```html
<html>
    <head>
```

```
            <title>This is PHP function</title>
        </head>
        <body>
            <?php
            class Vegetables {
              // these are the Properties
              public $vname;
              public $vcolor;

              // these are the Methods
              function set_name($vname) {
                $this->vname = $vname;
              }
              function get_name() {
                return $this->vname;
              }
            }
            $potato = new Vegetables();
            $beet = new Vegetables();
            $potato->set_name('Potato');
            $beet->set_name('Beet');

            echo $potato->get_name();
            echo "<br>";
            echo $beet->get_name();
            ?>
        </body>
</html>
```

$php main.php

```
<html>
      <head>
            <title>This is PHP function</title>
      </head>
      <body>
            Potato<br>Beet</body>
</html>
```

In the next code snippet, I'll add two more methods to the same vegetable class. I have added the methods to add color to the object.

```
<html>
    <head>
        <title>This is PHP function</title>
    </head>
    <body>
        <?php
        class Vegetables {
          // these are the Properties
          public $vname;
          public $vcolor;

          // these are the Methods
          function set_name($vname) {
            $this->vname = $vname;
          }
          function get_name() {
            return $this->vname;
          }
          function set_color($vcolor) {
            $this->vcolor = $vcolor;
          }
          function get_color() {
            return $this->vcolor;
          }
        }
        $potato = new Vegetables();
        $beet = new Vegetables();
        $potato->set_name('Potato');
        $potato->set_color('Red');
        $beet->set_name('Beet');
        $beet->set_color('Blue');
        echo $potato->get_name();
        echo "Color: " . $potato->get_color();
        echo "<br>";
        echo $beet->get_name();
        echo "<br>";
```

```
            echo "Color: " . $beet->get_color();
            ?>
        </body>
</html>
```

$php main.php

```
<html>
      <head>
            <title>This is PHP function</title>
      </head>
      <body>
            PotatoColor: Red<br>Beet<br>Color:
      Blue</body>
</html>
```

Vegetable Class

When you have to define a class, you should declare the properties right at the top. There is no need to declare the variables. You can just use them as you deem fit without declaring them. However, it is better to declare the properties when you are creating a class. This makes classes much easier to decipher. If you leave it out, it will be considered a poor programming practice. You will need a keyword for each property declaration; that's how you can access them.

The first keyword is public through which you can access the property from outside the class from another class or the script. The second keyword is private through which you cannot access the property from outside of the class. The third keyword is protected through which you cannot access it from the outside.

The Constructor Function

A PHP constructor allows you to initialize the properties of an object upon the creation of the object. PHP will call the function when you make an object from a class.

```
<html>
    <head>
        <title>This is PHP function</title>
    </head>
    <body>
        <?php
        class Vegetables {
          // these are the Properties
          public $vname;
          public $vcolor;

          // these are the Methods
          function __construct($vname) {
            $this->vname = $vname;
          }
          function get_name() {
            return $this->vname;
          }
        }
        $potato = new Vegetables("Potato");
        echo $potato->get_name();
        ?>
    </body>
</html>
```

$php main.php

```
<html>
    <head>
        <title>This is PHP function</title>
    </head>
```

```
        <body>
             Potato</body>
</html>
```

I am going to add another feature of color to the existing code. Take a look at the changes in the __constructor.

```
<html>
    <head>
         <title>This is PHP function</title>
    </head>
    <body>
         <?php
         class Vegetables {
           // these are the Properties
           public $vname;
           public $vcolor;
           public $vweight;
           public $vshape;

           // these are the Methods
           function __construct($vname, $vcolor, $vweight, $vshape) {
              $this->vname = $vname;
              $this->vcolor = $vcolor;
              $this->vweight = $vweight;
              $this->vshape = $vshape;
           }
           function get_name() {
              return $this->vname;
           }
           function get_color() {
              return $this->vcolor;
           }
           function get_weight() {
              return $this->vweight;
           }
           function get_shape() {
              return $this->vshape;
```

81

```php
    }
}
$potato = new Vegetables("Potato", " Brown", " 50", " round");
echo $potato->get_name();
echo "<br>";
echo $potato->get_color();
echo "<br>";
echo $potato->get_weight();
echo "<br>";
echo $potato->get_shape();

$beet = new Vegetables(" Beet" , " Red ", " 50 ", " round ");
echo $beet->get_name();
echo "<br>";
echo $beet->get_color();
echo "<br>";
echo $beet->get_weight();
echo "<br>";
echo $beet->get_shape();

$tomato = new Vegetables(" Tomato " , " Red ", " 100 ", " round ");
echo $tomato->get_name();
echo "<br>";
echo $tomato->get_color();
echo "<br>";
echo $tomato->get_weight();
echo "<br>";
echo $tomato->get_shape();

$turnip = new Vegetables(" Turnip " , "White ", " 150 ", " round ");
echo $turnip->get_name();
echo "<br>";
echo $turnip->get_color();
echo "<br>";
echo $turnip->get_weight();
```

```
            echo "<br>";
            echo $turnip->get_shape();
            ?>
    </body>
</html>
```

$php main.php

```
<html>
    <head>
        <title>This is PHP function</title>
    </head>
    <body>
        Potato<br> Brown<br> 50<br> round
        Beet<br> Red<br> 50<br> round Tomato<br>
        Red<br> 100<br> round
        Turnip<br>White<br>150<br>round</body>
</html>
```

Destructor

You have to call a destructor when an object gets destructed or the script stops or exits. If you get the opportunity to create a __destruct() function, PHP will call it at the end of the script. Just like the constructor function, destructor also starts with two underscores.

```
<html>
    <head>
        <title>This is PHP function</title>
    </head>
    <body>
        <?php
        class Vegetables {
          // these are the Properties
          public $vname;
          public $vcolor;
```

```php
            // these are the Methods
            function __construct($vname, $vcolor) {
               $this->vname = $vname;
               $this->vcolor = $vcolor;
            }
            function __destruct() {
               echo "The vegetable is {$this->vname} and the color is {$this->vcolor}.";

            }
         }
         $potato = new Vegetables("Potato", "Brown");

         $beet = new Vegetables(" Beet" , "Red");
         ?>
      </body>
</html>
```

$php main.php

```
<html>
      <head>
            <title>This is PHP function</title>
      </head>
      <body>
      </body>
</html>
```

The vegetable is Beet and the color is Red. The vegetable is Potato and the color is Brown.

PHP Access Modifiers

PHP properties and methods tend to have access modifiers that can control where and how they can be accessed. Generally, there are three access modifiers, namely public, protected, and private.

With the public modifier, a particular method or property can be accessed from anywhere. With the protected modifier, a method or property can be accessed inside a class and by the classes derived from that class. With the private modifier, a method of property can be accessed only inside a class.

In this example, I have added three different access modifiers to the above three properties. If you set the name property, you will succeed in doing that. However, if you set the weight and color properties, you will see a fatal error.

```
<html>
    <head>
        <title>This is PHP</title>
    </head>
    <body>
        <?php
        class Vegetable {
          public $vname;
          protected $vcolor;
          private $vweight;
        }

        $beet = new Vegetable();
        $beet->vname = 'Beet'; // OK
        $beet->vcolor = 'Purplish Red'; // This will trigger an ERROR
        $beet->vweight = '500'; // This will trigger an ERROR
        ?>
    </body>
</html>
```

$php main.php

```
<html>
    <head>
        <title>This is PHP</title>
    </head>
<body>
```

PHP Fatal error: Uncaught Error: Cannot access protected property Vegetable::$vcolor in /home/cg/root/271113/main.php:15

Stack trace:

```
#0 {main}
   thrown in /home/cg/root/271113/main.php on
line 15
```

In this next example, I will add access modifiers to the two methods. If you try to call the set_vcolor() or the set_vweight() functions, it will give fatal error, because the two have been designated as protected and private. This will happen despite the fact that we have made the properties public.

```
<html>
    <head>
        <title>This is PHP</title>
    </head>
    <body>
        <?php
        class Vegetable {
          public $vname;
          public $vcolor;
          public $vweight;

          function set_vname($n) {  // Now this is
          a public function (default)
             $this->vname = $n;
          }
```

```
            protected function set_vcolor($n) { //
        This is a protected function
            $this->vcolor = $n;
            }
            private function set_vweight($n) { // a
        This is a private function
            $this->vweight = $n;
            }
        }

        $beet = new Vegetable();
        $beet->vname = 'Beet'; // OK
        $beet->vcolor = 'Purplish Red'; // This
        will trigger an ERROR
        $beet->vweight = '500'; // This will
        trigger an ERROR
        ?>
    </body>
</html>
```

Inheritance

Inheritance in OOP means when a class is derived from another class. The child class tends to inherit almost all the protected and public methods and properties from the parent class. It also can have its own methods and properties. You can define it by using the *extends* keyword.

```
<html>
    <head>
        <title>This is PHP</title>
    </head>
    <body>
        <?php
        class Vegetable {
          public $vname;
          public $vcolor;
          public function __construct($vname,
        $vcolor) {
```

```
            $this->vname = $vname;
            $this->vcolor = $vcolor;
         }
         public function intro() {
            echo "The vegetable is {$this->vname}
         and its color is {$this->vcolor}.";
         }
      }

      // The beet is inherited from Vegetable
      class Beet extends Vegetable {
         public function themessage() {
            echo "Does beet taste like fruit or
         vegetable? ";
         }
      }
      $beet = new Beet("Beet", "purplish red");
      $beet->themessage();
      $beet->intro();
      ?>
   </body>
</html>
```

$php main.php

```
<html>
      <head>
            <title>This is PHP</title>
      </head>
<body>
```

Does beet taste like fruit or vegetable? The vegetable is Beet and its color is purplish red.</body>

```
      </html>
```

As Beet is inherited from the Vegetable class, it can use the vname and vcolor properties and the other methods that I have filled in the Vegetable class. It also has its own method namely *themessage*.

In the next example, I will turn the function from the main class from public to protected. You will see a fatal error on the screen of your editor.

```
<html>
    <head>
        <title>This is PHP</title>
    </head>
    <body>
        <?php
        class Vegetable {
          public $vname;
          public $vcolor;
          public function __construct($vname, $vcolor) {
             $this->vname = $vname;
             $this->vcolor = $vcolor;
          }
          protected function intro() {
             echo "The vegetable is {$this->vname} and its color is {$this->vcolor}.";
          }
        }

        // The beet is inherited from Vegetable
        class Beet extends Vegetable {
          public function themessage() {
             echo "Does beet taste like fruit or vegetable? ";
          }
        }
        $beet = new Beet("Beet", "purplish red");
        $beet->themessage();
        $beet->intro();
```

```
            ?>
        </body>
</html>
```

$php main.php

```
<html>
    <head>
        <title>This is PHP</title>
    </head>
<body>
```

Does beet taste like fruit or vegetable?

PHP Fatal error: Uncaught Error: Call to protected method Vegetable::intro() from context '' in /home/cg/root/271113/main.php:27

Stack trace:

```
#0 {main}
    thrown in /home/cg/root/271113/main.php on line 27
```

There is a solution to fix this problem. We can call the protected method intro() from inside the derived class.

```
<html>
    <head>
        <title>This is PHP</title>
    </head>
    <body>
        <?php
        class Vegetable {
          public $vname;
          public $vcolor;
```

```php
      public function __construct($vname, $vcolor) {
        $this->vname = $vname;
        $this->vcolor = $vcolor;
      }
      protected function intro() {
        echo "The vegetable is {$this->vname} and its color is {$this->vcolor}.";
      }
    }

    // The beet is inherited from Vegetable
    class Beet extends Vegetable {
      public function themessage() {
        echo "Does beet taste like fruit or vegetable? ";
        // I am calling protected method now from within the derived class
        $this -> intro();
      }
    }
    $beet = new Beet("Beet", "purplish red");
    $beet->themessage();
    ?>
  </body>
</html>
```

$php main.php

```html
<html>
    <head>
        <title>This is PHP</title>
    </head>
    <body>
        Does beet taste like fruit or vegetable? The vegetable is Beet and its color is purplish red.</body>
</html>
```

Overriding Inheritance

The inherited methods can be overridden if you redefine them in the child class. In the following example, I will override them.

```
<html>
    <head>
        <title>This is PHP</title>
    </head>
    <body>
        <?php
        class Vegetable {
          public $vname;
          public $vcolor;
          public function __construct($vname, $vcolor) {
             $this->vname = $vname;
             $this->vcolor = $vcolor;
          }
          public function intro() {
             echo "The vegetable is {$this->vname} and its color is {$this->vcolor}.";
          }
        }

        // The beet is inherited from Vegetable
        class Beet extends Vegetable {
            public $vweight;
            public function __construct($vname, $vcolor, $vweight) {
               $this->vname = $vname;
               $this->vcolor = $vcolor;
               $this->vweight = $vweight;
        }
          public function intro() {
             echo "The vegetable is {$this->vname} and its color is {$this->vcolor}, and its size is {$this->vweight}";
          }
```

```
            }
            $beet = new Beet("Beet", "purplish red",
            500);
            $beet->intro();
            ?>
    </body>
</html>
```

$php main.php

```
<html>
    <head>
        <title>This is PHP</title>
    </head>
    <body>
            The vegetable is Beet and its color is
            purplish red, and its size is 500</body>
</html>
```

You can prevent overriding by inserting the final keyword in the script.

```
<html>
    <head>
        <title>This is PHP</title>
    </head>
    <body>
            <?php
            final class Vegetable {
              public $vname;
              public $vcolor;
              public function __construct($vname,
            $vcolor) {
                 $this->vname = $vname;
                 $this->vcolor = $vcolor;
              }
              public function intro() {
```

93

```
            echo "The vegetable is {$this->vname}
        and its color is {$this->vcolor}.";
          }
        }

        // The beet is inherited from Vegetable
        class Beet extends Vegetable {
            public $vweight;
            public function __construct($vname,
        $vcolor, $vweight) {
            $this->vname = $vname;
            $this->vcolor = $vcolor;
            $this->vweight = $vweight;
        }
          public function intro() {
            echo "The vegetable is {$this->vname}
        and its color is {$this->vcolor}, and its
        size is {$this->vweight}";
          }
        }
        $beet = new Beet("Beet", "purplish red",
        500);
        $beet->intro();
        ?>
    </body>
</html>
```

$php main.php

PHP Fatal error: Class Beet may not inherit from final class (Vegetable) in /home/cg/root/271113/main.php on line 30

Abstract Class

When you are inheriting from the abstract class, the child class method ought to be defined with the same name and a less restricted access modifier. If the abstract method is defined as protected, the child class method needs to be defined either as public or protected, however not private. The number and type of the required arguments ought to be the same.

```
<html>
    <head>
        <title>This is PHP</title>
    </head>
    <body>
        <?php
        abstract class Vegetable {
          public $vname;
          public $vcolor;
          public function __construct($vname, $vcolor) {
             $this->vname = $vname;
             $this->vcolor = $vcolor;
          }
          abstract public function intro() : string;
        }

        // The beet is inherited from Vegetable
        class Beet extends Vegetable {
          public function intro() : string {
             return "The vegetable is $this->vname and its color is $this->vcolor";
          }
        }

        class Onion extends Vegetable {
          public function intro() : string {
             return "The vegetable is $this->vname and its color is $this->vcolor";
          }
        }

        class Pumpkin extends Vegetable {
          public function intro() : string {
```

```php
    return "The vegetable is $this->vname
and its color is $this->vcolor";
  }
}

class Radish extends Vegetable {
  public function intro() : string {
    return "The vegetable is $this->vname
and its color is $this->vcolor";
  }
}

class Tomato extends Vegetable {
  public function intro() : string {
    return "The vegetable is $this->vname
and its color is $this->vcolor";
  }
}
$beet = new Beet("Beet", "purplish red",
500);
echo $beet->intro();
echo "<br>";

$onion = new Onion("Onion", "white", 50);
echo $onion->intro();
echo "<br>";

$pumpkin = new Pumpkin("Pumpkin",
"green", 100);
echo $pumpkin->intro();
echo "<br>";

$radish = new Radish("Radish", "red",
250);
echo $radish->intro();
echo "<br>";

$tomato = new Tomato("Tomato", "red and
green", 200);
```

```
            echo $tomato->intro();
            echo "<br>";
            ?>
        </body>
</html>
```

$php main.php

```
<html>
      <head>
            <title>This is PHP</title>
      </head>
      <body>
            The vegetable is Beet and its color is
            purplish red<br>The vegetable is Onion
            and its color is white<br>The vegetable
            is Pumpkin and its color is green<br>The
            vegetable is Radish and its color is
            red<br>The vegetable is Tomato and its
            color is red and green<br></body>
</html>
```

Abstract Class Examples

```
<html>
      <head>
            <title>This is PHP</title>
      </head>
      <body>
            <?php
            abstract class ParentClass {
              // This is an Abstract method with an
            argument
               abstract protected function
            theprefixName($name);
            }
```

```php
          class ChildClass extends ParentClass {
            public function theprefixName($vname) {
              if ($vname == "John Snow") {
                $theprefix = "Mister.";
              } else-if ($vname == "Jane Snow") {
                $theprefix = "Mrs.";
              } else {
                $theprefix = "";
              }
              return "{$theprefix} {$vname}";
            }
          }
          $class = new ChildClass;
          echo $class->theprefixName("John Snow");
          echo "<br>";
          echo $class->theprefixName("Jane Snow");
          ?>
    </body>
</html>
```

$php main.php

```
<html>
      <head>
            <title>This is PHP</title>
      </head>
<body>
            Mister. John Snow<br>Mrs. Jane
      Snow</body>
</html>
```

Here is another example of the same abstract class.

```
<html>
      <head>
            <title>This is PHP</title>
      </head>
```

```php
        <body>
            <?php
            abstract class ParentClass {
              // This is an Abstract method with an argument
              abstract protected function theprefixName($name);
            }

            class ChildClass extends ParentClass {
              public function theprefixName($vname, $theseparator = ".", $vgreet = "My dear ") {
                  if ($vname == "John Snow") {
                    $theprefix = "Mister.";
                  } else-if ($vname == "Jane Snow") {
                    $theprefix = "Mrs.";
                  } else {
                    $thoprefix = "";
                  }
                  return "{$vgreet}{$theprefix}{$theseparator} {$vname}";
                }
            }
            $class = new ChildClass;
            echo $class->theprefixName("John Snow");
            echo "<br>";
            echo $class->theprefixName("Jane Snow");
            ?>
        </body>
</html>
```

$php main.php

```
<html>
    <head>
        <title>This is PHP</title>
</head>
```

```
        <body>
            My dear  Mister.. John Snow<br>My dear
        Mrs.. Jane Snow</body>
</html>
```

Chapter Six

PHP Forms and File Handling

The PHP superglobal variables like $_POST and $_GET are generally used for the collection of form-data. This chapter will walk you through the creation and handling of PHP forms. I will start with a simple HTML form that has two input fields. It will also have a submit button for the users to fill in the information and press the submit button to complete the transaction. You can build a web application and integrate the form in that to retrieve certain information from the users that you need.

```
<html>
    <body>
        <form action="Wewelcomeyou.php" method="post">
        Name: <input type="text" name="Please enter your name"><br>
        E-mail: <input type="text" name="Please enter your email"><br>
        <input type="submit">
        </form>
    </body>
</html>
```

When a user fills out the form and enters the submit button, the data proceeds for processing to a PHP file that is named as Wewelcomeyou.php. The form is dispatched with the HTTP POST method. If you want to display your submitted data, you can simply echo the variables.

If you use the $GET method to send the form, it will be visible to everyone. All names and values will be displayed in the URL. It also has limits on the size of the information you want to send. Variables will be displayed in the URL, so it will be impossible to create a bookmark on the page.

You also can use the POST method to create a form, but the problem is that in this method, the information will be visible to others.

In the next code example, you will see new variables that will help you add error messages for all the required fields. There will also be an if else statement for each of the $_POST variable. It will check if $_POST variable is empty or not, because if it is not, you will be see an error message, packed in different error variables. It will send the user input data through the test_input() function.

```
<html>
    <head>
        <title>This is PHP</title>
    </head>
    <body>
<?php
// you ought to define variables and set them to empty values
    $pnameErr = $pemailErr = $pgenderErr = $pwebsiteErr = "";
    $pname = $pemail = $pgender = $pcomment = $pwebsite = "";
        if ($_SERVER["REQUEST_METHOD"] == "POST")
        {
           if (empty($_POST["name"])) {
             $pnameErr = "You will be requiring a name";
            } else {
             $pname = test_input($_POST["name"]);
            }
```

```php
      if (empty($_POST["email"])) {
        $pemailErr = "You will be requiring an Email";
      } else {
        $pemail = test_input($_POST["email"]);
      }

      if (empty($_POST["website"])) {
        $pwebsite = "";
      } else {
        $pwebsite = test_input($_POST["website"]);
      }

      if (empty($_POST["comment"])) {
        $pcomment = "";
      } else {
        $pcomment = test_input($_POST["comment"]);
      }

      if (empty($_POST["gender"])) {
        $pgenderErr = "You will have to enter your Gender";
      } else {
        $pgender = test_input($_POST["gender"]);
      }
    }
    ?>
  </body>
</html>
```

PHP File Handling

Exception handling is something that programmers label as the toughest part of software development. Errors such as program bug, network failure, and database failure create a bunch of serious problems for programmers. Developers ought to make decisions regarding errors that pop up during the writing phase, add checks to detect a failure and invoke the perfect function for managing it. Programmers also ought to make sure that the programs work normally after handling the error.

Exceptions help you write powerful programs without the need to write 'if' statements in the code blocks. This means that you can always minimize the codes that you ought to write.

PHP forms are of many types. The most basic that you can add to your web application is the PHP Date() function. The required format parameter of the function tends to specify how you can format the date and time. Take a look at some characters that you can use for dates. The 'd' character will represent the days of the month from 01 to 31. The 'm' character represents months of the year from 01 to 12. The 'y' parameter represents four digits of the year. The 'l' represents the day of the week.

```
<html>
    <head>
        <title>This is PHP</title>
    </head>
    <body>
        <?php
        echo "The date is " . date("Y/m/d") . "<br>";
        echo "The date is " . date("Y.m.d") . "<br>";
        echo "The date is " . date("Y-m-d") . "<br>";
        echo "The date is " . date("l");
```

```
            ?>
        </body>
</html>
```

$php main.php

```
<html>
    <head>
        <title>This is PHP</title>
    </head>
    <body>
        The date is 2020/06/23<br>The date is
        2020.06.23<br>The date is 2020-06-
        23<br>The date is Tuesday</body>
</html>
```

When the new year starts, you can update the copyright year of your web application by the following method.

```
&copy; 2020-<?php echo date("Y");?>
```

Here is the example of how you can ask PHP to estimate the exact date even four months in forward.

```
<html>
    <head>
        <title>This is PHP</title>
    </head>
    <body>
        <?php
        $d=strtotime(" tomorrow ");
        echo date("m-d-y h:i:sa", $d) . "<br>";

        $d=strtotime(" next Friday ");
        echo date(" m-d-y h:i:sa ", $d) . "<br>";

        $d=strtotime(" +4 Months ");
```

```
            echo date(" m-d-y h:i:sa ", $d) . "<br>";

            $d=strtotime(" +8 Months ");
            echo date(" m-d-y h:i:sa ", $d) . "<br>";

            $d=strtotime("+1 Month ");
            echo date(" m-d-y h:i:sa ", $d) . "<br>";

            $d=strtotime(" next Wednesday ");
            echo date(" m-d-y h:i:sa ", $d) . "<br>";
        ?>
    </body>
</html>
```

$php main.php

```
<html>
    <head>
        <title>This is PHP</title>
    </head>
    <body>
        06-24-20 12:00:00am<br> 06-26-20
        12:00:00am <br> 10-23-20 05:13:14am <br>
        02-23-21 05:13:14am <br> 07-23-20
        05:13:14am <br> 06-24-20 12:00:00am
        <br></body>
</html>
```

More Examples

```
<html>
    <head>
        <title>This is PHP</title>
    </head>
    <body>
        <?php
        $thestartdate = strtotime("Friday");
```

```php
            $theenddate = strtotime("+36 weeks",
            $thestartdate);

            while ($thestartdate < $theenddate) {
              echo date("M d Y", $thestartdate) .
            "<br>";
              $thestartdate = strtotime("+1 day",
            $thestartdate);
            }
            ?>
      </body>
</html>
```

$php main.php

```
<html>
      <head>
            <title>This is PHP</title>
      </head>
<body>
            Jun 26 2020<br>Jun 27 2020<br>Jun 28
            2020<br>Jun 29 2020<br>Jun 30 2020<br>Jul
            01 2020<br>Jul 02 2020<br>Jul 03
            2020<br>Jul 04 2020<br>Jul 05 2020<br>Jul
            06 2020<br>Jul 07 2020<br>Jul 08
            2020<br>Jul 09 2020<br>Jul 10 2020<br>Jul
            11 2020<br>Jul 12 2020<br>Jul 13
            2020<br>Jul 14 2020<br>Jul 15 2020<br>Jul
            16 2020<br>Jul 17 2020<br>Jul 18
            2020<br>Jul 19 2020<br>Jul 20 2020<br>Jul
            21 2020<br>Jul 22 2020<br>Jul 23
            2020<br>Jul 24 2020<br>Jul 25 2020<br>Jul
            26 2020<br>Jul 27 2020<br>Jul 28
            2020<br>Jul 29 2020<br>Jul 30 2020<br>Jul
            31 2020<br>Aug 01 2020<br>Aug 02
            2020<br>Aug 03 2020<br>Aug 04 2020<br>Aug
            05 2020<br>Aug 06 2020<br>Aug 07
```

2020
Aug 08 2020
Aug 09 2020
Aug 10 2020
Aug 11 2020
Aug 12 2020
Aug 13 2020
Aug 14 2020
Aug 15 2020
Aug 16 2020
Aug 17 2020
Aug 18 2020
Aug 19 2020
Aug 20 2020
Aug 21 2020
Aug 22 2020
Aug 23 2020
Aug 24 2020
Aug 25 2020
Aug 26 2020
Aug 27 2020
Aug 28 2020
Aug 29 2020
Aug 30 2020
Aug 31 2020
Sep 01 2020
Sep 02 2020
Sep 03 2020
Sep 04 2020
Sep 05 2020
Sep 06 2020
Sep 07 2020
Sep 08 2020
Sep 09 2020
Sep 10 2020
Sep 11 2020
Sep 12 2020
Sep 13 2020
Sep 14 2020
Sep 15 2020
Sep 16 2020
Sep 17 2020
Sep 18 2020
Sep 19 2020
Sep 20 2020
Sep 21 2020
Sep 22 2020
Sep 23 2020
Sep 24 2020
Sep 25 2020
Sep 26 2020
Sep 27 2020
Sep 28 2020
Sep 29 2020
Sep 30 2020
Oct 01 2020
Oct 02 2020
Oct 03 2020
Oct 04 2020
Oct 05 2020
Oct 06 2020
Oct 07 2020
Oct 08 2020
Oct 09 2020
Oct 10 2020
Oct 11 2020
Oct 12 2020
Oct 13 2020
Oct 14 2020
Oct 15 2020
Oct 16 2020
Oct 17 2020
Oct 18 2020
Oct 19 2020
Oct 20 2020
Oct 21 2020
Oct 22 2020
Oct 23 2020
Oct 24 2020
Oct 25 2020
Oct 26 2020
Oct 27 2020
Oct 28 2020
Oct 29 2020
Oct 30 2020
Oct 31 2020
Nov 01 2020
Nov 02 2020
Nov 03 2020
Nov 04 2020
Nov 05 2020
Nov 06 2020
Nov 07 2020
Nov 08 2020
Nov 09 2020
Nov 10 2020
Nov 11 2020
Nov 12 2020
Nov

13 2020
Nov 14 2020
Nov 15 2020
Nov 16 2020
Nov 17 2020
Nov 18 2020
Nov 19 2020
Nov 20 2020
Nov 21 2020
Nov 22 2020
Nov 23 2020
Nov 24 2020
Nov 25 2020
Nov 26 2020
Nov 27 2020
Nov 28 2020
Nov 29 2020
Nov 30 2020
Dec 01 2020
Dec 02 2020
Dec 03 2020
Dec 04 2020
Dec 05 2020
Dec 06 2020
Dec 07 2020
Dec 08 2020
Dec 09 2020
Dec 10 2020
Dec 11 2020
Dec 12 2020
Dec 13 2020
Dec 14 2020
Dec 15 2020
Dec 16 2020
Dec 17 2020
Dec 18 2020
Dec 19 2020
Dec 20 2020
Dec 21 2020
Dec 22 2020
Dec 23 2020
Dec 24 2020
Dec 25 2020
Dec 26 2020
Dec 27 2020
Dec 28 2020
Dec 29 2020
Dec 30 2020
Dec 31 2020
Jan 01 2021
Jan 02 2021
Jan 03 2021
Jan 04 2021
Jan 05 2021
Jan 06 2021
Jan 07 2021
Jan 08 2021
Jan 09 2021
Jan 10 2021
Jan 11 2021
Jan 12 2021
Jan 13 2021
Jan 14 2021
Jan 15 2021
Jan 16 2021
Jan 17 2021
Jan 18 2021
Jan 19 2021
Jan 20 2021
Jan 21 2021
Jan 22 2021
Jan 23 2021
Jan 24 2021
Jan 25 2021
Jan 26 2021
Jan 27 2021
Jan 28 2021
Jan 29 2021
Jan 30 2021
Jan 31 2021
Feb 01 2021
Feb 02 2021
Feb 03 2021
Feb 04 2021
Feb 05 2021
Feb 06 2021
Feb 07 2021
Feb 08 2021
Feb 09 2021
Feb 10 2021
Feb 11 2021
Feb 12 2021
Feb 13 2021
Feb 14 2021
Feb 15 2021
Feb 16 2021
Feb 17 2021
Feb 18

```
            2021<br>Feb 19 2021<br>Feb 20 2021<br>Feb
            21 2021<br>Feb 22 2021<br>Feb 23
            2021<br>Feb 24 2021<br>Feb 25 2021<br>Feb
            26 2021<br>Feb 27 2021<br>Feb 28
            2021<br>Mar 01 2021<br>Mar 02 2021<br>Mar
            03 2021<br>Mar 04 2021<br></body>
</html>
```

The Include Factor

In order to include the footer file in the page, you ought to use the include statement.

```
<html>
      <head>
            <title>This is PHP</title>
      </head>
      <body>
            <h1>You are welcome to this home
            page!</h1>
            <p>I would love to help in making your
            business successful.</p>
            <p>Would like to consider a look into our
            discount offers.</p>
            <?php include 'footer.php';?>

            ?>
      </body>
</html>
```

File Handling

File handling is an integral part of web applications. More often you ought to open and then process a particular file for a number of tasks. There are a number of functions for reading, creating, editing, and uploading files. When you are trying to manipulate files, you should be careful lest you should inflict significant damage on the program. The most common errors are editing a wrong file, filling a hard drive with waste data and deleting the content by accident.

The readfile() Function

The PHP readfile() function tends to read a file and then write it to the output buffer.

```
<html>
    <head>
        <title>This is PHP</title>
    </head>
    <body>
        <?php
        echo readfile("mycountrieslist.txt");
        ?>
    </body>
</html>
```

You can add other keywords like fread() and fclose() to read a file and close it after that.

Exception Handling

An exception is a particular object that reveals an error or any other unexpected behavior of the PHP script. PHP functions or classes are usually carry many exceptions. Exceptions are a better way to stop a particular function when it comes across the data that it cannot use.

The throw statement permits a user defined function or a method to throw a particular function. When a particular exception is thrown, the following code will not be executed. It the exception is never caught, a fatal error will occur.

```
<html>
    <head>
        <title>This is PHP</title>
    </head>
```

```
<body>
    <?php
    function thedivide($thedividend,
    $thedivisor) {
      if($thedivisor == 0) {
        throw new Exception("This is a
    division by zero");
      }
      return $thedividend / $thedivisor;
    }

    try {
      echo thedivide(10, 0);
    } catch(Exception $e) {
      echo "This is something unable to be
    divided.";
    }
    ?>
</body>
</html>
```

$php main.php

```
<html>
    <head>
        <title>This is PHP</title>
    </head>
<body>
        This is something unable to be
    divided.</body>
</html>
```

In the following code example, I will change the values.

```
<html>
    <head>
        <title>This is PHP</title>
```

```
        </head>
        <body>
            <?php
            function thedivide($thedividend,
            $thedivisor) {
              if($thedivisor == 0) {
                throw new Exception("This is a
            division by zero");
              }
              return $thedividend / $thedivisor;
            }

            try {
              echo thedivide(10, 50);
            } catch(Exception $e) {
              echo "This is something unable to be
            divided.";
            }
            ?>
        </body>
</html>
```

$php main.php

```
<html>
        <head>
            <title>This is PHP</title>
        </head>
        <body>
            0.2</body>
</html>
```

See the following example with a change in values.

```
<html>
        <head>
            <title>This is PHP</title>
```

```
        </head>
        <body>
            <?php
            function thedivide($thedividend,
            $thedivisor) {
              if($thedivisor == 0) {
                throw new Exception("This is a
            division by zero");
              }
              return $thedividend / $thedivisor;
            }

            try {
              echo thedivide(10, 100);
                } catch(Exception $e) {
                  echo "This is something unable to
              be divided.";
                }
            ?>
        </body>
</html>
```

$php main.php

```
<html>
    <head>
        <title>This is PHP</title>
    </head>
    <body>
        0.1</body>
</html>
```

The try…catch…finally statement can also be used to detect some exceptions. The code that rests in the finally block will run no matter an *exception* is caught or not. If you add *finally* to the code, the *catch* block will be optional.

```
<html>
    <head>
        <title>This is PHP</title>
    </head>
    <body>
    <?php
    function thedivide($thedividend, $thedivisor) {
      if($thedivisor == 0) {
        throw new Exception("It will be a division by zero");
      }
      return $thedividend / $thedivisor;
    }

    try {
      echo thedivide(200, 10);
    } catch(Exception $e) {
      echo "  This is unable to be divided. ";
        } finally {
          echo "  This means that the process is complete.";
        }
        ?>
    </body>
</html>
```

$php main.php

```
<html>
    <head>
        <title>This is PHP</title>
</head>
        <body>
        20  This means that the process is complete.</body>
</html>
```

115

See the example in which the figures are not divisible.

```
<html>
    <head>
        <title>This is PHP</title>
    </head>
    <body>
        <?php
        function thedivide($thedividend, $thedivisor) {
          if($thedivisor == 7) {
            throw new Exception("It will be a division by zero");
          }
          return $thedividend / $thedivisor;
        }

        try {
          echo thedivide(17, 7);
        } catch(Exception $e) {
          echo " This is unable to be divided. ";
        } finally {
            echo " This means that the process is complete.";
        }
        ?>
    </body>
</html>
```

$php main.php

```
<html>
    <head>
        <title>This is PHP</title>
    </head>
    <body>
```

```
           This is unable to be divided.   This
     means that the process is
     complete.</body>
</html>
```

See another example.

```
<html>
    <head>
        <title>This is PHP</title>
    </head>
    <body>
        <?php
        function thedivide($thedividend,
        $thedivisor) {
          if($thedivisor == 19) {
            throw new Exception("It will be a
        division by zero");
          }
          return $thedividend / $thedivisor;
        }

        try {
          echo thedivide(5276, 47);
        } catch(Exception $e) {
          echo "  This is unable to be divided.
        ";
        } finally {
          echo "  This means that the process is
        complete.";
        }
        ?>
    </body>
</html>
```

$php main.php

```
<html>
     <head>
          <title>This is PHP</title>
     </head>
<body>
     112.25531914894   This means that the process is
     complete.</body>
</html>
```

Chapter Seven

MySQL Basics

Lots of websites demand a backend database that would contain the information that the web pages display to the user or store the information that the users would fill in the website. MySQL is a highly popular database that can be used on websites. It was developed as a small yet fast system for websites. MySQL is specifically popular to be used in websites that are scripted in PHP. In short, MySQL and PHP tend to work well together.

MySQL contains a MySQL server, a bunch of utility programs that would aid in the administration of MySQL databases, and some supporting software that the MySQL server needs. The MySQL server is considered as the manager of the database system. It can handle all the database instructions.

MySQL is dubbed as a Relational Database System (RDBMS). The MySQL server tends to manage multiple databases right at the same time. Many people might in control of different databases that are managed by one MySQL server. Each of them has a structure that can hold the data. Generally, a database tends to exist without data. You can store data inside of a database in the form of tables. The tables ought to be created before you can add data to your database. Create an empty database in the start and fill it in with data later on. Each row of a table acts as an entity such as a book or a project. Each column carries an item of information about an entity like the name of a book or a customer.

A database contains one or more tables, and each table can be identified by a particular name. Just like a normal table, MySQL table contains columns and rows. I will be using a database in these scripts.

MySQL Queries

It is mostly English. It is made up of English phrases and sentences. You don't have to see through and learn an arcane tech language to write the queries. The first word of the statement is its name. It is an action word that tells MySQL what you want it to do. These statements will be discussed in this chapter.

You cannot install or uninstall MySQL on your system as it runs on a web hosting computer. You can access data on MySQL through an account.

SQL SELECT

The first on the line is the SQL select statement. I have a demo database that is currently perched in the database. The table that is in your database is as under.

CustomerID	Customer Name	Contact Number	Secret Code	Country
1.	Emily Jack	55779034	45	United States
2.	Jason Austin	34568988	2	United Kingdom
3.	Amanda McMahon	34578899	1	Ireland

4.	Victoria Ann	23768800	67	Germany
5.	Simon Wiz	45327899	9	United States
6.	Tracy Drupal	23897609	8	France
7.	Emilia Tim	45890093	3	Italy
8.	Tyson Jackson	34980900	2	Sweden

So this is what we have, and we can access it by using SQL statements. If you want to display the complete table, you can use the following statement.

```
SELECT * FROM Members;
```

In this statement, Members is the name of the abovementioned table. The rest belongs to SQL. The Select statement is very interesting if you use it properly. You can use it to display different columns of the table. For example, you work at a firm that holds the database mentioned above. Your boss asks you to print out the list of the names of the members and their country of origin only, leaving the rest of the database. You can do that in a matter of seconds by using the following statement.

Customer ID	Customer Name	Contact Number	Secret Code	Country
1.	Emily Jack	55779034	45	United States
2.	Jason Austin	34568988	2	United Kingdom

3.	Amanda McMahon	34578899	1	Ireland
4.	Victoria Ann	23768800	67	Germany
5.	Simon Wiz	45327899	9	United States
6.	Tracy Drupal	23897609	8	France
7.	Emilia Tim	45890093	3	Italy
8.	Tyson Jackson	34980900	2	Sweden

```
SELECT CustomerName, Country FROM Members;
```

Customer Name	Country
Emily Jack	United States
Jason Austin	United Kingdom
Amanda McMahon	Ireland
Victoria Ann	Germany
Simon Wiz	United States
Tracy Drupal	France
Emilia Tim	Italy
Tyson Jackson	Sweden

DISTINCT Statement

The SELECT DISTINCT statement is often used to return the distinct values only. Sometimes, a column contains duplicate values, and you only wish to list just the distinct values. In this situation, you can opt for the SELECT DISTINCT statement. When we display the table using the simple SELECT statement, it displays all the values that are in the columns without discriminating about the duplicate entries. The DISTINCT statement only displays distinct values from the columns. The demo table is as under.

Customer ID	Customer Name	Contact Number	Secret Code	Country
1.	Emily Jack	55779034	45	United States
2.	Jason Austin	34568988	2	United Kingdom
3.	Amanda McMahon	34578899	1	Ireland
4.	Victoria Ann	23768800	67	Germany
5.	Simon Wiz	45327899	9	United States
6.	Tracy Drupal	23897609	8	France
7.	Emilia Tim	45890093	3	Italy
8.	Tyson Jackson	34980900	2	Sweden

```
SELECT DISTINCT Country FROM Members;
```

Country
United States
United Kingdom
Ireland
Germany
France
Italy
Sweden

The United States was duplicated, but here only a single entry is on display.

WHERE Clause

This particular statement selects the members from a particular location that you will mention. Let's revise the table in the database before applying the SQL statement on the same.

Customer ID	Customer Name	Contact Number	Secret Code	Country
1.	Emily Jack	55779034	45	United States
2.	Jason Austin	34568988	2	United Kingdom

3.	Amanda McMahon	34578899	1	Ireland
4.	Victoria Ann	23768800	67	Germany
5.	Simon Wiz	45327899	9	United States
6.	Tracy Drupal	23897609	8	France
7.	Emilia Tim	45890093	3	Italy
8.	Tyson Jackson	34980900	2	Sweden
9.	Tom Dick	45980999	4	United States
10.	Dane harry	47889933	0	United States

This is the table in the database.

```
SELECT * FROM Members
WHERE Country= 'United States';
```

Customer ID	Customer Name	Contact Number	Secret Code	Country
1.	Emily Jack	55779034	45	United States
5.	Simon Wiz	45327899	9	United

				States
9.	Tom Dick	45980999	4	United States
10.	Dane harry	47889933	0	United States

Take a look at another example of the WHERE statement.

```
SELECT * FROM Members
WHERE CustomerID=1;
WHERE CustomerID=2;
WHERE CustomerID=3;
WHERE CustomerID=4;
WHERE CustomerID=5;
WHERE CustomerID=6;
WHERE CustomerID=7;
```

Customer ID	Customer Name	Contact Number	Secret Code	Country
1.	Emily Jack	55779034	45	United States
2.	Jason Austin	34568988	2	United Kingdom
3.	Amanda McMahon	34578899	1	Ireland.
4.	Victoria Ann	23768800	67	Germany
5.	Simon Wiz	45327899	9	United States

| 6. | Tracy Drupal | 23897609 | 8 | France |
| 7. | Emilia Tim | 45890093 | 3 | Italy |

AND Statement

The following statement will select all the fields from the table Members where the country is the United States, or Secret Code is 7. I will make a few changes in the database table and display it before executing the statement.

Customer ID	Customer Name	Contact Number	Secret Code	Country
1.	Emily Jack	55779034	45	United States
2.	Jason Austin	34568988	7	United Kingdom
3.	Amanda McMahon	34578899	7	Ireland
4.	Victoria Ann	23768800	67	Germany
5.	Simon Wiz	45327899	7	United States
6.	Tracy Drupal	23897609	7	France
7.	Emilia Tim	45890093	3	Italy

8.	Tyson Jackson	34980900	7	Sweden
9.	Tom Dick	45980999	4	United States
10.	Dane harry	47889933	0	United States

Here is the statement.

```
SELECT * FROM Members
WHERE Members= 'United States' AND
SecretCode=7;
```

Customer ID	Customer Name	Contact Number	Secret Code	Country
1.	Emily Jack	55779034	45	United States
2.	Jason Austin	34568988	7	United Kingdom
3.	Amanda McMahon	34578899	7	Ireland
5.	Simon Wiz	45327899	7	United States
6.	Tracy Drupal	23897609	7	France

8.	Tyson Jackson	34980900	7	Sweden
9.	Tom Dick	45980999	4	United States
10.	Dane harry	47889933	0	United States

There is another amazing statement known as the OR statement. It allows you to be choosy when you retrieve data from the database.

```
SELECT * FROM Members
WHERE Country= 'United States' OR SecretCode= 7;
```

Customer ID	Customer Name	Contact Number	Secret Code	Country
1.	Emily Jack	55779034	45	United States
2.	Jason Austin	34568988	7	United Kingdom
3.	Amanda McMahon	34578899	7	Ireland
5.	Simon Wiz	45327899	7	United States
6.	Tracy Drupal	23897609	7	France

8.	Tyson Jackson	34980900	7	Sweden
9.	Tom Dick	45980999	4	United States
10.	Dane harry	47889933	0	United States

Take another example.

```
SELECT * FROM Members
WHERE Members= 'United States' OR CustomerID = 2;
```

Customer ID	Customer Name	Contact Number	Secret Code	Country
1.	Emily Jack	55779034	45	United States
2.	Jason Austin	34568988	7	United Kingdom
5.	Simon Wiz	45327899	7	United States
9.	Tom Dick	45980999	4	United States
10.	Dane harry	47889933	0	United States

If you want to leave one entry and retrieve all the others, you can use the NOT statement in the script.

```
SELECT * FROM Members
WHERE NOT Country= 'Sweden';
```

Customer ID	Customer Name	Contact Number	Secret Code	Country
1.	Emily Jack	55779034	45	United States
2.	Jason Austin	34568988	7	United Kingdom
3.	Amanda McMahon	34578899	7	Ireland
4.	Victoria Ann	23768800	67	Germany
5.	Simon Wiz	45327899	7	United States
6.	Tracy Drupal	23897609	7	France
7	Emilia Tim	15890093	3	Italy
9.	Tom Dick	45980999	4	United States
10.	Dane harry	47889933	0	United States

Combining AND, OR and NOT

You can combine the three statements to make the working more precise and neat. The following statements will select different fields from Members where the country is the United States, and the name is Emilia Jackson.

Here is the table.

Customer ID	Customer Name	Contact Number	Secret Code	Country
1.	Emilia Jackson	55779034	45	United States
2.	Jason Austin	34568988	7	United Kingdom
3.	Amanda McMahon	34578899	7	Ireland
4.	Victoria Ann	23768800	67	Germany
5.	Harry Styles	45327899	7	United States
6.	Tracy Drupal	23897609	7	France
7.	Emilia Tim	45890093	3	Italy
8.	Tyson Jackson	34980900	7	Sweden
9.	Emilia Jackson	45980999	4	United States
10.	Harry Styles	47889933	0	United States

Let's write the SQL statement.

```
SELECT * FROM Members
WHERE Members= 'United States' AND
(CustomerName= 'Emilia Jackson' OR
CustomerName= 'Harry Styles');
```

Customer ID	Customer Name	Contact Number	Secret Code	Country
1.	Emilia Jackson	55779034	45	United States
5.	Harry Styles	45327899	7	United States
9.	Emilia Jackson	45980999	4	United States
10.	Harry Styles	47889933	0	United States

AND NOT Statements

You can use AND NOT statements to exclude two different entries from the table and then display it on the screen or print it out. The table, in its entirety, is as under:

Customer ID	Customer Name	Contact Number	Secret Code	Country
1.	Emilia Jackson	55779034	45	United States
2.	Jason Austin	34568988	7	United Kingdom

3.	Amanda McMahon	34578899	7	Ireland
4.	Victoria Ann	23768800	67	Germany
5.	Harry Styles	45327899	7	United States
6.	Tracy Drupal	23897609	7	France
7.	Emilia Tim	45890093	3	Italy
8.	Tyson Jackson	34980900	7	Sweden
9.	Emilia Jackson	45980999	4	United States
10.	Harry Styles	47889933	0	United States

```
SELECT * FROM Members
WHERE NOT Country= 'Sweden' AND NOT Country= 'United Kingdom'
```

Customer ID	Customer Name	Contact Number	Secret Code	Country
1.	Emilia Jackson	55779034	45	United States
3.	Amanda McMahon	34578899	7	Ireland
4.	Victoria Ann	23768800	67	Germany

5.	Harry Styles	45327899	7	United States
6.	Tracy Drupal	23897609	7	France
7.	Emilia Tim	45890093	3	Italy
9.	Emilia Jackson	45980999	4	United States
10.	Harry Styles	47889933	0	United States

ORDER BY Keyword

You can use the ORDER BY keyword to sort out the results either in the ascending or the descending order. The ORDER BY keyword will sort the records in the ascending order by default. To sort it in the descending order, you can use the DESC keyword.

Here is the table in the present form.

Customer ID	Customer Name	Contact Number	Secret Code	Country
1.	Emilia Jackson	55779034	45	United States
2.	Jason Austin	34568988	7	United Kingdom
3.	Amanda McMahon	34578899	7	Ireland
4.	Victoria Ann	23768800	67	Germany

5.	Harry Styles	45327899	7	United States
6.	Tracy Drupal	23897609	7	France
7.	Emilia Tim	45890093	3	Italy
8.	Tyson Jackson	34980900	7	Sweden
9.	Emilia Jackson	45980999	4	United States
10.	Harry Styles	47889933	0	United States

Here is the statement you have to type in.

```
SELECT * FROM Members
ORDER BY Members;
```

Customer ID	Customer Name	Contact Number	Secret Code	Country
6.	Tracy Drupal	23897609	7	France
4.	Victoria Ann	23768800	67	Germany
3.	Amanda McMahon	34578899	7	Ireland
7.	Emilia Tim	45890093	3	Italy
8.	Tyson Jackson	34980900	7	Sweden

2.	Jason Austin	34568988	7	United Kingdom
1.	Emilia Jackson	55779034	45	United States
5.	Harry Styles	45327899	7	United States
9.	Emilia Jackson	45980999	4	United States
10.	Harry Styles	47889933	0	United States

Here is the result in a perfectly ascending order. However, you can reverse the order by using the DESC keyword in the SQL statement. It will select all the entries and shuffle it up into descending order by picking up the country column. This is the current form of the table.

Customer ID	Customer Name	Contact Number	Secret Code	Country
1.	Emilia Jackson	55779034	45	United States
2.	Jason Austin	34568988	7	United Kingdom
3.	Amanda McMahon	34578899	7	Ireland
4.	Victoria Ann	23768800	67	Germany
5.	Harry Styles	45327899	7	United States

6.	Tracy Drupal	23897609	7	France
7.	Emilia Tim	45890093	3	Italy
8.	Tyson Jackson	34980900	7	Sweden
9.	Emilia Jackson	45980999	4	United States
10.	Harry Styles	47889933	0	United States

```
SELECT * FROM Members
ORDER BY Members DESC;
```

Customer ID	Customer Name	Contact Number	Secret Code	Country
1.	Emilia Jackson	55779034	45	United States
9.	Emilia Jackson	45980999	4	United States
10.	Harry Styles	47889933	0	United States
5.	Harry Styles	45327899	7	United States
2.	Jason Austin	34568988	7	United Kingdom
8.	Tyson Jackson	34980900	7	Sweden

3.	Amanda McMahon	34578899	7	Ireland
7.	Emilia Tim	45890093	3	Italy
4.	Victoria Ann	23768800	67	Germany
6.	Tracy Drupal	23897609	7	France

It is also possible that you set two different columns in the ascending and descending order or the two in the ascending order.

```
SELECT * FROM Members
ORDER BY CustomerName, Country;
```

INSERT INTO Statements

By using this statement, you can update the database whenever you like. We have a table in the database, and we will update it accordingly. Let's take a look at the table.

Customer ID	Customer Name	Contact Number	Secret Code	Country
1.	Emilia Jackson	55779034	45	United States
2.	Jason Austin	34568988	7	United Kingdom
3.	Amanda McMahon	34578899	7	Ireland
4.	Victoria Ann	23768800	67	Germany
5.	Harry Styles	45327899	7	United States

6.	Tracy Drupal	23897609	7	France
7.	Emilia Tim	45890093	3	Italy
8.	Tyson Jackson	34980900	7	Sweden
9.	Emilia Jackson	45980999	4	United States
10.	Harry Styles	47889933	0	United States

```
INSERT INTO Members (CustomerID, CustomerName,
ContactNumber, SecretCode, Country)
Values ('11', 'Haddy,' '45789809', '7', 'United
States');
```

Customer ID	Customer Name	Contact Number	Secret Code	Country
1.	Emilia Jackson	55779034	45	United States
2.	Jason Austin	34568988	7	United Kingdom
3.	Amanda McMahon	34578899	7	Ireland
4.	Victoria Ann	23768800	67	Germany
5.	Harry Styles	45327899	7	United States
6.	Tracy Drupal	23897609	7	France
7.	Emilia Tim	45890093	3	Italy

8.	Tyson Jackson	34980900	7	Sweden
9.	Emilia Jackson	45980999	4	United States
10.	Harry Styles	47889933	0	United States
11.	Haddy	45789809	7	United States

```
INSERT INTO Members (CustomerID, CustomerName,
ContactNumber, SecretCode, Country)
Values ('12', 'Sylvia,' '15769091', '9',
'United States');
```

Customer ID	Customer Name	Contact Number	Secret Code	Country
1.	Emilia Jackson	55779034	45	United States
2.	Jason Austin	34568988	7	United Kingdom
3.	Amanda McMahon	34578899	7	Ireland
4.	Victoria Ann	23768800	67	Germany
5.	Harry Styles	45327899	7	United States
6.	Tracy Drupal	23897609	7	France
7.	Emilia Tim	45890093	3	Italy

8.	Tyson Jackson	34980900	7	Sweden
9.	Emilia Jackson	45980999	4	United States
10.	Harry Styles	47889933	0	United States
11.	Haddy	45789809	7	United States
12	Sylvia	15769091	9	United States

You can be selective and add data only to specific columns of the table.

```
INSERT INTO Members (CustomerName, SecretCode, Country)
Values ('Tane,' '5', 'Sweden')
```

Customer ID	Customer Name	Contact Number	Secret Code	Country
1.	Emilia Jackson	55779034	45	United States
2.	Jason Austin	34568988	7	United Kingdom
3.	Amanda McMahon	34578899	7	Ireland
4.	Victoria Ann	23768800	67	Germany

5.	Harry Styles	45327899	7	United States
6.	Tracy Drupal	23897609	7	France
7.	Emilia Tim	45890093	3	Italy
8.	Tyson Jackson	34980900	7	Sweden
9.	Emilia Jackson	45980999	4	United States
10.	Harry Styles	47889933	0	United States
11.	Haddy	45789809	7	United States
12	Sylvia	15769091	9	United States
	Tane		5	Sweden

Update Table

The following SQL statement will update the CustomerID 1 by replacing it with a new CustomerName and new SecretCode. Here is what the table looks like now.

Customer ID	Customer Name	Contact Number	Secret Code	Country
1.	Emilia	55779034	45	United

	Jackson			States
2.	Jason Austin	34568988	7	United Kingdom
3.	Amanda McMahon	34578899	7	Ireland
4.	Victoria Ann	23768800	67	Germany
5.	Harry Styles	45327899	7	United States
6.	Tracy Drupal	23897609	7	France
7.	Emilia Tim	45890093	3	Italy
8.	Tyson Jackson	34980900	7	Sweden
9.	Emilia Jackson	45980999	4	United States
10.	Harry Styles	47889933	0	United States
11.	Haddy	45789809	7	United States
12	Sylvia	15769091	9	United States

UPDATE Members

```
SET CustomerName = 'Fanny', SecretCode = '007'
WHERE CustomerID = 1;
```

Customer ID	Customer Name	Contact Number	Secret Code	Country
1.	Fanny	55779034	007	United States
2.	Jason Austin	34568988	7	United Kingdom
3.	Amanda McMahon	34578899	7	Ireland
4.	Victoria Ann	23768800	67	Germany
5.	Harry Styles	45327899	7	United States
6.	Tracy Drupal	23897609	7	France
7.	Emilia Tim	45890093	3	Italy
8.	Tyson Jackson	34980900	7	Sweden
9.	Emilia Jackson	45980999	4	United States
10.	Harry Styles	47889933	0	United States

| 11. | Haddy | 45789809 | 7 | United States |
| 12 | Sylvia | 15769091 | 9 | United States |

Here is another example in which I have changed the columns.

UPDATE Members

```
SET CustomerName = 'Milton', Country =
'Bolivia'
WHERE CustomerID = 5;
```

Customer ID	Customer Name	Contact Number	Secret Code	Country
1.	Fanny	55779034	007	United States
2.	Jason Austin	34568988	7	United Kingdom
3.	Amanda McMahon	34578899	7	Ireland
4.	Victoria Ann	23768800	67	Germany
5.	Milton	45327899	7	Bolivia
6.	Tracy Drupal	23897609	7	France
7.	Emilia Tim	45890093	3	Italy
8.	Tyson Jackson	34980900	7	Sweden

9.	Emilia Jackson	45980999	4	United States
10.	Harry Styles	47889933	0	United States
11.	Haddy	45789809	7	United States
12	Sylvia	15769091	9	United States

The WHERE statement is amazing. It allows you to change multiple records at the same time. For example, you can use it to update different sets. See the following example.

UPDATE Members

```
SET CustomerName= 'Marlow'
WHERE SecretCode= '7'
```

Customer ID	Customer Name	Contact Number	Secret Code	Country
1.	Fanny	55779034	007	United States
2.	Marlow	34568988	7	United Kingdom
3.	Marlow	34578899	7	Ireland
4.	Victoria Ann	23768800	67	Germany
5.	Marlow	45327899	7	United States

6.	Marlow	23897609	7	France
7.	Emilia Tim	45890093	3	Italy
8.	Marlow	34980900	7	Sweden
9.	Emilia Jackson	45980999	4	United States
10.	Harry Styles	47889933	0	United States
11.	Marlow	45789809	7	United States
12	Sylvia	15769091	9	United States

You can make this change by using the country column.

UPDATE Members

```
SET CustomerName= 'Dom Carry'
WHERE Country= 'United States';
```

Customer ID	Customer Name	Contact Number	Secret Code	Country
1.	Dom Carry	55779034	007	United States
2.	Marlow	34568988	7	United Kingdom
3.	Marlow	34578899	7	Ireland

4.	Victoria Ann	23768800	67	Germany
5.	Dom Carry	45327899	7	United States
6.	Marlow	23897609	7	France
7.	Emilia Tim	45890093	3	Italy
8.	Marlow	34980900	7	Sweden
9.	Dom Carry	45980999	4	United States
10.	Dom Carry	47889933	0	United States
11.	Dom Carry	45789809	7	United States
12	Dom Carry	15769091	9	United States

You should be extremely careful about using the WHERE clause because if you miss out on including it, you will end up updating all the records in the database. This will turn out to be nothing less than a disaster for your database. See how you can make the blunder that could ruin your database. The table is as under.

Customer ID	Customer Name	Contact Number	Secret Code	Country
1.	Fanny	55779034	007	United States
2.	Marlow	34568988	7	United

				Kingdom
3.	Marlow	34578899	7	Ireland
4.	Victoria Ann	23768800	67	Germany
5.	Marlow	45327899	7	United States
6.	Marlow	23897609	7	France
7.	Emilia Tim	45890093	3	Italy
8.	Marlow	34980900	7	Sweden
9.	Emilia Jackson	45980999	4	United States
10.	Harry Styles	47889933	0	United States
11.	Marlow	45789809	7	United States
12	Sylvia	15769091	9	United States

UPDATE Members

```
SET CustomerName= 'Dom Carry'
```

Customer ID	Customer Name	Contact Number	Secret Code	Country
1.	Dom Carry	55779034	007	United States
2.	Dom Carry	34568988	7	United Kingdom
3.	Dom Carry	34578899	7	Ireland
4.	Dom Carry	23768800	67	Germany
5.	Dom Carry	45327899	7	United States
6.	Dom Carry	23897609	7	France
7.	Dom Carry	45890093	3	Italy
8.	Dom Carry	34980900	7	Sweden
9.	Dom Carry	45980999	4	United States
10.	Dom Carry	47889933	0	United States
11.	Dom Carry	45789809	7	United States
12	Dom Carry	15769091	9	United States

DELETE

Just like with any document, you can delete records from a database. The database that I will be using is as under:

Customer ID	Customer Name	Contact Number	Secret Code	Country
1.	Fanny	55779034	007	United States
2.	Marlow	34568988	7	United Kingdom
3.	Marlow	34578899	7	Ireland
4.	Victoria Ann	23768800	67	Germany
5.	Marlow	45327899	7	United States
6.	Marlow	23897609	7	France
7.	Emilia Tim	45890093	3	Italy
8.	Marlow	34980900	7	Sweden
9.	Emilia Jackson	45980999	4	United States
10.	Harry Styles	47889933	0	United States
11.	Marlow	45789809	7	United States
12	Sylvia	15769091	9	United States

The statement to delete a specific record entry from the table is as under.

```
DELETE FROM Members WHERE CustomerName = 'Sylvia';
```

Customer ID	Customer Name	Contact Number	Secret Code	Country
1.	Fanny	55779034	007	United States
2.	Marlow	34568988	7	United Kingdom
3.	Marlow	34578899	7	Ireland
4.	Victoria Ann	23768800	67	Germany
5.	Marlow	45327899	7	United States
6.	Marlow	23897609	7	France
7.	Emilia Tim	45890093	3	Italy
8.	Marlow	34980900	7	Sweden
9.	Emilia Jackson	45980999	4	United States
10.	Harry Styles	47889933	0	United States
11.	Marlow	45789809	7	United States

Try out another by another record.

```
DELETE FROM Members WHERE Country = 'United
Kingdom.'
```

Customer ID	Customer Name	Contact Number	Secret Code	Country
1.	Fanny	55779034	007	United States
3.	Marlow	34578899	7	Ireland
4.	Victoria Ann	23768800	67	Germany
5.	Marlow	45327899	7	United States
6.	Marlow	23897609	7	France
7.	Emilia Tim	45890093	3	Italy
8.	Marlow	34980900	7	Sweden
9.	Emilia Jackson	45980999	4	United States
10.	Harry Styles	47889933	0	United States
11.	Marlow	45789809	7	United States
12	Sylvia	15769091	9	United States

SELECT TOP

The SELECT TOP statement is used to retrieve the top records that you need to return, leaving the rest of the table hidden. You can use it on large-sized tables that have thousands of records. This is useful because if you return a large number of records, it will impact your performance.

Customer ID	Customer Name	Contact Number	Secret Code	Country
1.	Fanny	55779034	007	United States
2.	Marlow	34568988	7	United Kingdom
3.	Marlow	34578899	7	Ireland
4.	Victoria Ann	23768800	67	Germany
5.	Marlow	45327899	7	United States
6.	Marlow	23897609	7	France
7.	Emilia Tim	45890093	3	Italy
8.	Marlow	34980900	7	Sweden
9.	Emilia Jackson	45980999	4	United States
10.	Harry Styles	47889933	0	United States

| 11. | Marlow | 45789809 | 7 | United States |
| 12 | Sylvia | 15769091 | 9 | United States |

```
SELECT TOP 6 * FROM Members;
```

Customer ID	Customer Name	Contact Number	Secret Code	Country
1.	Fanny	55779034	007	United States
2.	Marlow	34568988	7	United Kingdom
3.	Marlow	34578899	7	Ireland
4.	Victoria Ann	23768800	67	Germany
5.	Marlow	45327899	7	United States
6.	Marlow	23897609	7	France

You also can use the LIMIT clause to specify the number of records that you want to see. Take a look at the following example.

```
SELECT * FROM Members
LIMIT 8;
```

Customer ID	Customer Name	Contact Number	Secret Code	Country
1.	Fanny	55779034	007	United States
2.	Marlow	34568988	7	United Kingdom
3.	Marlow	34578899	7	Ireland
4.	Victoria Ann	23768800	67	Germany
5.	Marlow	45327899	7	United States
6.	Marlow	23897609	7	France
7.	Emilia Tim	45890093	3	Italy
8.	Marlow	34980900	7	Sweden

An interesting statement that you can use in a state in which you have to work speedily is the PERCENT clause. If you don't know how many records are there in the table, you can slice off the table through the middle, carving out the bottom 50 percent and displaying the top 50 percent. Here is the table in the database.

Customer ID	Customer Name	Contact Number	Secret Code	Country
1.	Fanny	55779034	007	United States
2.	Marlow	34568988	7	United Kingdom

3.	Marlow	34578899	7	Ireland
4.	Victoria Ann	23768800	67	Germany
5.	Marlow	45327899	7	United States
6.	Marlow	23897609	7	France
7.	Emilia Tim	45890093	3	Italy
8.	Marlow	34980900	7	Sweden
9.	Emilia Jackson	45980999	4	United States
10.	Harry Styles	47889933	0	United States
11.	Marlow	45789809	7	United States
12	Sylvia	15769091	9	United States

Here is the TOP PERCENT statement.

```
SELECT TOP 50 PERCENT * FROM Members;
```

Customer ID	Customer Name	Contact Number	Secret Code	Country
1.	Fanny	55779034	007	United States
2.	Marlow	34568988	7	United Kingdom

3.	Marlow	34578899	7	Ireland
4.	Victoria Ann	23768800	67	Germany
5.	Marlow	45327899	7	United States
6.	Marlow	23897609	7	France

COUNT()

You can use the COUNT () statement to count the number of values in a specific column. Here is the table that you can use to apply the count statement.

Customer ID	Customer Name	Contact Number	Secret Code	Country
1.	Fanny	55779034	007	United States
2.	Marlow	34568988	7	United Kingdom
3.	Marlow	34578899	7	Ireland
4.	Victoria Ann	23768800	67	Germany
5.	Marlow	45327899	7	United States
6.	Marlow	23897609	7	France
7.	Emilia Tim	45890093	3	Italy
8.	Marlow	34980900	7	Sweden

9.	Emilia Jackson	45980999	4	United States
10.	Harry Styles	47889933	0	United States
11.	Marlow	45789809	7	United States
12	Sylvia	15769091	9	United States

```
SELECT COUNT(CustomerID)
FROM Members;
```

The answer will be 12, as there are a total of 12 entries in this column.

% Wildcard

The below-mentioned SQL statements will select the countries with 'es' at the end. The demo table looks like this.

Customer ID	Customer Name	Contact Number	Secret Code	Country
1.	Fanny	55779034	007	United States
2.	Marlow	34568988	7	United Kingdom
3.	Marlow	34578899	7	Ireland
4.	Victoria Ann	23768800	67	Germany

5.	Marlow	45327899	7	United States
6.	Marlow	23897609	7	France
7.	Emilia Tim	45890093	3	Italy
8.	Marlow	34980900	7	Sweden
9.	Emilia Jackson	45980999	4	United States
10.	Harry Styles	47889933	0	United States
11.	Marlow	45789809	7	United States
12	Sylvia	15769091	9	United States

Now I will apply the % Wildcard on the table.

```
SELECT * FROM Members
WHERE Country LIKE '%es%';
```

Customer ID	Customer Name	Contact Number	Secret Code	Country
1.	Fanny	55779034	007	United States
5.	Marlow	45327899	7	United States
9.	Emilia Jackson	45980999	4	United States

10.	Harry Styles	47889933	0	United States
11.	Marlow	45789809	7	United States
12	Sylvia	15769091	9	United States

In the following example, I will try to retrieve the records that end with 'om.' See the demo table.

Customer ID	Customer Name	Contact Number	Secret Code	Country
1.	Fanny	55779034	007	United States
2.	Marlow	34568988	7	United Kingdom
3.	Marlow	34578899	7	Ireland
4.	Victoria Ann	23768800	67	Germany
5.	Marlow	45327899	7	United States
6.	Marlow	23897609	7	France
7.	Emilia Tim	45890093	3	Italy
8.	Marlow	34980900	7	Sweden
9.	Emilia Jackson	45980999	4	United States

10.	Harry Styles	47889933	0	United States
11.	Marlow	45789809	7	United States
12	Sylvia	15769091	9	United States

Here is the statement.

```
SELECT * FROM Members
WHERE Country LIKE '%om%.'
```

Customer ID	Customer Name	Contact Number	Secret Code	Country
2.	Marlow	34568988	7	United Kingdom

Charlist Wildcard

In the following statements, you will be able to display the records by listing the first character of a particular country. Here is how to do that.

Customer ID	Customer Name	Contact Number	Secret Code	Country
1.	Fanny	55779034	007	United States
2.	Marlow	34568988	7	United Kingdom
3.	Marlow	34578899	7	Ireland

4.	Victoria Ann	23768800	67	Germany
5.	Marlow	45327899	7	United States
6.	Marlow	23897609	7	France
7.	Emilia Tim	45890093	3	Italy
8.	Marlow	34980900	7	Sweden
9.	Emilia Jackson	45980999	4	United States
10.	Harry Styles	47889933	0	United States
11.	Marlow	45789809	7	United States
12	Sylvia	15769091	9	United States

Now let us write the statement.

```
SELECT * FROM Members
WHERE Country LIKE ' [isu]%;
```

Customer ID	Customer Name	Contact Number	Secret Code	Country
1.	Fanny	55779034	007	United States
2.	Marlow	34568988	7	United Kingdom
3.	Marlow	34578899	7	Ireland

5.	Marlow	45327899	7	United States
7.	Emilia Tim	45890093	3	Italy
8.	Marlow	34980900	7	Sweden
9.	Emilia Jackson	45980999	4	United States
10.	Harry Styles	47889933	0	United States
11.	Marlow	45789809	7	United States
12	Sylvia	15769091	9	United States

Let's bring that table back into its original form and then try to display the countries that start with 'u' only. Here is the table.

Customer ID	Customer Name	Contact Number	Secret Code	Country
1.	Fanny	55779034	007	United States
2.	Marlow	34568988	7	United Kingdom
3.	Marlow	34578899	7	Ireland
4.	Victoria Ann	23768800	67	Germany
5.	Marlow	45327899	7	United States

6.	Marlow	23897609	7	France
7.	Emilia Tim	45890093	3	Italy
8.	Marlow	34980900	7	Sweden
9.	Emilia Jackson	45980999	4	United States
10.	Harry Styles	47889933	0	United States
11.	Marlow	45789809	7	United States
12	Sylvia	15769091	9	United States

```
SELECT * FROM Members
WHERE Country LIKE '[u]%;
```

Customer ID	Customer Name	Contact Number	Secret Code	Country
1.	Fanny	55779034	007	United States
2.	Marlow	34568988	7	United Kingdom
5.	Marlow	45327899	7	United States
9.	Emilia Jackson	45980999	4	United States

10.	Harry Styles	47889933	0	United States
11.	Marlow	45789809	7	United States
12	Sylvia	15769091	9	United States

IN Operator

This operator will make things a lot easier for you. It will select all the customers who live in a particular country. You can just type in the name of the country and display the records of the same.

Customer ID	Customer Name	Contact Number	Secret Code	Country
1.	Fanny	55779034	007	United States
2.	Marlow	34568988	7	United Kingdom
3.	Marlow	34578899	7	Ireland
4.	Victoria Ann	23768800	67	Germany
5.	Marlow	45327899	7	United States
6.	Marlow	23897609	7	France
7.	Emilia Tim	45890093	3	Italy
8.	Marlow	34980900	7	Sweden

9.	Emilia Jackson	45980999	4	United States
10.	Harry Styles	47889933	0	United States
11.	Marlow	45789809	7	United States
12	Sylvia	15769091	9	United States

Here is the statement.

```
SELECT * FROM Members
WHERE Country IN ('The United States,' 'United
Kingdom,' 'Italy')
```

Customer ID	Customer Name	Contact Number	Secret Code	Country
1.	Fanny	55779034	007	United States
2.	Marlow	34568988	7	United Kingdom
5.	Marlow	45327899	7	United States
7.	Emilia Tim	45890093	3	Italy
9.	Emilia Jackson	45980999	4	United States
10.	Harry Styles	47889933	0	United States

| 11. | Marlow | 45789809 | 7 | United States |
| 12 | Sylvia | 15769091 | 9 | United States |

There is another SQL statement that helps you filter the records by blocking entries from a certain country. The following SQL statement will block all customers that are not located in Germany, Sweden, and France. Take a look at the demo table in the present form.

Customer ID	Customer Name	Contact Number	Secret Code	Country
1.	Fanny	55779034	007	United States
2.	Marlow	34568988	7	United Kingdom
3.	Marlow	34578899	7	Ireland
4.	Victoria Ann	23768800	67	Germany
5.	Marlow	45327899	7	United States
6.	Marlow	23897609	7	France
7.	Emilia Tim	45890093	3	Italy
8.	Marlow	34980900	7	Sweden
9.	Emilia Jackson	45980999	4	United States

10.	Harry Styles	47889933	0	United States
11.	Marlow	45789809	7	United States
12	Sylvia	15769091	9	United States

Here is the statement.

```
SELECT * FROM Members
WHERE Country NOT IN ('German,' 'Sweden,'
'France');
```

Customer ID	Customer Name	Contact Number	Secret Code	Country
1.	Fanny	55779034	007	United States
2.	Marlow	34568988	7	United Kingdom
3.	Marlow	34578899	7	Ireland
5.	Marlow	45327899	7	United States
7.	Emilia Tim	45890093	3	Italy
9.	Emilia Jackson	45980999	4	United States
10.	Harry Styles	47889933	0	United States

| 11. | Marlow | 45789809 | 7 | United States |
| 12 | Sylvia | 15769091 | 9 | United States |

SELECT INTO

In big organizations where data is huge, and there is always a danger of loss of data, you have to create multiple copies of it to store in the database. If you do it manually, it will take a big amount of time to create a perfect copy by filling in each record entry manually in the database. Moreover, on some occasions, the data is user-specific, which means that you cannot retrieve it easily. MySQL allows you to create as many copies of your data as you need to. Take a look at the following example.

Customer ID	Customer Name	Contact Number	Secret Code	Country
1.	Fanny	55779034	007	United States
2.	Marlow	34568988	7	United Kingdom
3.	Marlow	34578899	7	Ireland
4.	Victoria Ann	23768800	67	Germany
5.	Marlow	45327899	7	United States
6.	Marlow	23897609	7	France
7.	Emilia Tim	45890093	3	Italy

8.	Marlow	34980900	7	Sweden
9.	Emilia Jackson	45980999	4	United States
10.	Harry Styles	47889933	0	United States
11.	Marlow	45789809	7	United States
12	Sylvia	15769091	9	United States

Here is the statement:

```
SELECT * INTO MembersBackup2020
FROM Members;
```

Customer ID	Customer Name	Contact Number	Secret Code	Country
1.	Fanny	55779034	007	United States
2.	Marlow	34568988	7	United Kingdom
3.	Marlow	34578899	7	Ireland
4.	Victoria Ann	23768800	67	Germany
5.	Marlow	45327899	7	United States

6.	Marlow	23897609	7	France
7.	Emilia Tim	45890093	3	Italy
8.	Marlow	34980900	7	Sweden
9.	Emilia Jackson	45980999	4	United States
10.	Harry Styles	47889933	0	United States
11.	Marlow	45789809	7	United States
12	Sylvia	15769091	9	United States

Chapter Eight

Build Web Applications With PHP

You have seen how to program in PHP in the past chapters. You have seen how to create a program, set up conditionals, and create a loop, and much more. All that knowledge gives you the power to build PHP programs that would work well on the web. However, you can make them better and easier to use.

As the complexity of your programs rises, you will find a big number of require_once() and includes functions. Whenever you intend to create a new file or make something in a common function, you can add a require_once to the program.

If you direct a visitor to any URL like http://www.example.com/login.php, you can be able to use auto_prepend_file to need a helper file before the login.php code which is being run. This helper file has the power to start the session, offer multiple functions that you can use inside of the programs, or load multiple files. The auto_prepend_file function is an integral part of the php.ini file, but it is common to set it in the Apache configuration by using the php_value directive.

Prepend File

This section will explain that if you are looking forward to using sessions, you ought to call the session_start() function on all the pages that will be using sessions. This can be pretty tough if you are looking forward to tracking down sessions onto multiple PHP programs. You can then use an auto-prepend-file to call session_start.

Create two files; one will be the main file, and the other will contain a prepended function to start a particular session. Before you perform an exercise, you ought to ensure that .htaccess files are working or that you can alter the Apache webserver configuration. Make sure that you restart Apache if you are looking forward to making a change to the configuration.

Inside of the .htaccess file for the root of the document, you need to place the following code:

```
php_value auto_prepend_file "prepend.php"
```

You also can add the same line inside of the following script.

```
<Directory "/my/documentroot/path">
        php_value auto_prepend_file
     "/my/documentroot/path/prependfile.php"
</Directory>
```

If the root of the document is "/var/www" you should add the line after the <Directory "/var/www">.

Now open your text editor and create a fresh empty file. Inside of that file, you need to place the following code.

```
<html>
    <head>
        <title>This is PHP</title>
    </head>
    <body>
        <?php
         if (isset($_SESSION)) {
```

```
            print "Your Session starts!";
             } else {
              print "Your session did not
              start";
             }
        ?>
    </body>
</html>
```

$php main.php

```
<html>
    <head>
        <title>This is PHP</title>
    </head>
    <body>
        Your session did not start</body>
</html>
```

Now save the file as session.php inside of the document root. You can now open the web browser and enter http://localhost/session.php. You can now minimize the web browser and also create a new file in the text editor. Now place the following code inside of the new file.

```
<?php
    session_start();
?>
```

You can save this file as prepend.php in the document root. Inside of the browser, you can reload session.php file to view the same you created earlier on. If you receive a blank page or some kind of error on the browser, it means that the prepended file was not there. Go through the spellings to verify you have written them correctly.

If you see a page that says, 'Session has not started,' chances are that you Apache has not detected the auto_prepend_file directive. If you have placed the .htaccess file in the document root, you ought to make sure that Apache has read the .htaccess file. Read on or check with the hosting provider to see if .htaccess files have been allowed or not.

Some web server configurations have no room for .htaccess files. You can revise the Apache configuration to allow these files by changing AllowOverride to All for the directory, which has to read .htaccess file.

Classes For Efficiency

You can use classes to make your applications more efficient. You can create a class to define a user. After that, you can go on to adding functions, which are known as methods, to that user class for simple things that users might want to do on the web applications, such as updating the passwords. In the absence of classes, you might end up with multiple functions scattered around in the programs. This will complicate the code and make it look like a mess. Also, it will take a longer time to write the programs. If you write a program without classes, you will have to add a lot of functions to run the program properly. For example, if you want to write different user management programs with no classes, you will have to include in its different functions like setEmail, changePassword, addPermission, and many more.

Now you will have to merge that code with another one to add different roles to your programs. You can write these programs without adding classes, and they will share the same function names as your programs do. An example of the name is addPermission. When you aim at merging them, you will not have any confusion regarding the names.

If you, on the other hand, define the programs by using PHP classes, the addPermission function would not collide with other functions because the addPermission method is an integral part of the user class. You can recall it to create a user in a certain object-oriented manner, also known as instantiation, by using the New keyword. If the user class were labeled as User, you would need to instantiate like the following.

```
$user = new User;
```

Code Reuse

This also is one of the most important aspects of programming. A majority of programmers keep sets of functions or programs that they can frequently reuse whenever they need them. Most of the reusable codes are to kick off a program to save time that would be spent on creating the start. When you are building modern applications in PHP, you might find it useful to reuse your PHP code.

Functions

Functions are important parts of PHP coding. This section of the books expands on the idea of reusing functions in PHP programming. With the help of the auto-prepend_file, you can create a functions file that will be included in your PHP programs. These functions can be something as simple as kicking off a session or as complex as a login function. When you think you require a function in multiple files, you can use the auto_prepend file. One function that you can use in several places is something to convert a three-letter abbreviation of the name of a state into its full name. You can create a function and integrate it into the prepended PHP file. Open the prepend.php file that we have created in the previous section. Now clear the code outside of prepend.php and put it in the file.

```php
<html>
    <head>
        <title>This is PHP</title>
    </head>
    <body>
        <?php
         if (!isset($_SESSION)) {
         session_start();
         }
         function convertStateName($nstate) {
         $thestateList = array(
         "ALA" => "Alabama",
         "AKA" => "Alaska",
         "ARZ" => "Arizona",
         "ARK" => "Arkansas",
         "CAL" => "California",
         "COL" => "Colorado",
         "CTC" => "Connecticut",
         "DEL" => "Delaware",
         "FLO" => "Florida",
         "GGA" => "Georgia",
         "HWI" => "Hawaii",
         "IDA" => "Idaho",
         "ILI" => "Illinois",
         "IND" => "Indiana",
         "IOA" => "Iowa",
         "KAS" => "Kansas",
         "KTY" => "Kentucky",
         "LIA" => "Louisiana",
         "MAE" => "Maine",
         "MLD" => "Maryland",
         "MSA" => "Massachusetts",
         "MCI" => "Michigan",
         "MIN" -> "Minnesota",
         "MIS" => "Mississippi",
         "MOI" -> "Missouri",
         "MOT" => "Montana",
         "NEB" => "Nebraska",
         "NEV" => "Nevada",
```

```php
            "NHM" => "New Hampshire",
            "NJY" => "New Jersey",
            "NMX" => "New Mexico",
            "NYC" => "New York",
            "NCA" => "North Carolina",
            "NDA" => "North Dakota",
            "OHO" => "Ohio",
            "OKA" => "Oklahoma",
            "ORG" => "Oregon",
            "PSA" => "Pennsylvania",
            "RDI" => "Rhode Island",
            "SCA" => "South Carolina",
            "SDA" => "South Dakota",
            "TNS" => "Tennessee",
            "TXS" => "Texas",
            "UTA" => "Utah",
            "VNT" => "Vermont",
            "VGA" => "Virginia",
            "WSN" => "Washington",
            "WVG" => "West Virginia",
            "WIS" => "Wisconsin",
            "WYM" => "Wyoming"
            );
                if
                (array_key_exists($nstate,$thestate
                List)) {
                return $thestateList[$nstate];
                } else {
                return false;
                }
        }
        ?>
    </body>
</html>
```

Save it as prepend.php file in the document root. Now create another file with the following script.

```html
<html>
    <head>
        <title>This is PHP</title>
    </head>
    <body>
        <?php
         $stateAbbreviation = "WIS";
         print "The State abbreviation should be "
         . $stateAbbreviation . "<br>\n";
         $stateFull =
         convertState($stateAbbreviation);
         if ($stateFull) {
          print "The Full name of the state is " .
         $stateFull . "<br>\n";
             } else {
              print "The Full name of the state
             is not found for
             {$stateAbbreviation}<br>\n";
             }
         ?>
    </body>
</html>
```

You ought to save this file as stateabbreviation.php at the root of the document. Now open up the browser and open http://localhost/state.php. The code will check to see if the session has started or not. If not, it will display an error. The function convertState will accept some arguments to convert. The function will set up an array that will carry full names of the state. If you don't have a three-letter abbreviation, you will see an error on the screen. Otherwise, you will see the name of the state.

App Building

A majority of people use PHP to build different types of websites. This computer language allows programmers to create interactive web applications. A dynamic web application can collect data from the users by using HTML forms. The data procured from the users and saved in the database of the website remains confidential, which makes the security of the website a grave concern. PHP has features that allow programmers to harvest and securely store data. PHP contains everything a programmer needs to build web applications. All you need is to develop applications by using different features that are offered by this language. This chapter will walk you through the techniques of using PHP to build web applications.

PHP And HTML

There is no need to embed PHP codes into different HTML files. You can always create PHP files that don't possess any HTML elements. When you are creating web applications, you will combine these languages into a single file. Computer experts opine that PHP had been created for building websites. You can combine PHP and HTML, as you have seen in the past examples. These languages move side by side. Let's dissect the latest example that I have given in this book to understand how the two are combined.

```
<html>
    <head>
        <title>This is PHP</title>
    </head>
    <body>
        <?php
        abstract class ParentClass {
          // This is an Abstract method with an argument
            abstract protected function theprefixName($name);
}
        class ChildClass extends ParentClass {
            public function theprefixName($vname, $theseparator = ".", $vgreet = "My dear ") {
                if ($vname == "John Snow") {
```

```
                $theprefix = "Mister.";
            } else-if ($vname == "Jane Snow") {
                $theprefix = "Mrs.";
            } else {
                $theprefix = "";
            }
            return "{$vgreet}
        {$theprefix}{$theseparator} {$vname}";
            }
        }
        $class = new ChildClass;
        echo $class->theprefixName("John Snow");
        echo "<br>";
        echo $class->theprefixName("Jane Snow");
        ?>
    </body>
</html>
```

If you analyze the example, you can understand that after the body tags, the tag for PHP starts and it ends where the PHP script ends. In the example, <?php> signifies the beginning of PHP code that has been neatly embedded into the HTML body. The ?> marks the end of PHP script. You might notice that this example send the output through 'echo.'

User Input

Now that you have understood how PHP survives inside of an HTML file. All the modern web applications require space for user specified actions. Suppose there is an online bookstore which requires a login system and registration. Users ought to perform an action like entering the login credentials to reach inside of the online shop. This system requires HTML-based forms along with a storage for keeping the data secure in the storage. To create such an application, you need lots of things from each user during the registration process such as their usernames, passwords, and email IDs. Take a look at the following code that you will needing to create the application's user-oriented feature. There is no PHP in this example. You will only find

```html
<html>
    <head>
        <title>This is a Sign-up app</title></head>
    <body>
        <h1>You can freely Register Here</h1>
        <form method="get" action="thesignup.php">
        <table>
        <tr><td>You have to fill in your Email Address:</td>
        <td><input type="text" name="your email address"/> </td></tr>
        <tr><td>Name:</td>
        <td><input type="text" name="first_last_name"/></td></tr>
        <tr><td>This is the Space For Your Desired Password:</td>
        <td><input type="password" name="desiredpassword"/></td></tr>
        <tr>
        <td colspan ='5'>
        <input type="submit" name="signup" value="Sign up"/>
        </td>
        </tr>
        </table>
        </form>
    </body>
</html>
```

Building a PHP CMS

It can be safely said that every website that is up-to-date is using some kind of content management system (CMS). There are a number of great options that offer us CMS to power your WordPress or Drupal. However, a simple PHP class can help you create a proficient database. You can use PHP to connect your website to the database, display a form, save the data that flows in through the form, and display the data from the database.

Through the following class, you will get to know how MySQL and PHP will be interacting together. You will also learn about the basics of how to create a CMS.

Class Creation

The first step in the process is to build a PHP class and save it in the classCMS.php file. See how to create the class in PHP editor.

```
<html>
    <head>
        <title>This is PHP</title>
    </head>
    <body>
        <?php
        class thisisCMS {
            var $vhost;
            var $vusername;
            var $vpassword;
            var $vtable;

            public function dis_public() {

            }

            public function dis_admin() {

            }

            public function vwrite() {

            }
```

```
            public function vconnect() {

            }

            private function vbuildDB() {

            }
        }
    ?>
    </body>
</html>
```

A class for CMS has been created in PHP editor. There are four variables in the class and five different methods. I have used object-oriented programming to build this CMS app because it helps to keep the code clean in big projects. It is also easier to approach and practice.

The four variables will be used for connecting the code to the database. They will act as a bridge to access the database on a server. I have left them empty for now. I will not move on to the database and construct it with a PHP method.

```
private function vbuildDB() {
    $sql = <<<MySQL_QUERY
        CREATE TABLE IF NOT EXISTS testDB (
            titleVARCHAR(150),
            bodytext    TEXT,
            created     VARCHAR(100)
        )
    MySQL_QUERY;

    return mysql_query($sql);
}
```

There is a MySQL command in the function that will check the database to verify if testDB exists or not. If it does, it will pass a notification of success and, if not, it will create a table and assign three columns that would hold the data. The next step is to create a function that will connect to the database.

```
public function vconnect() {
    mysql_connect($this->vhost,$this->vusername,$this->vpassword) or die("I am unable to connect. " . mysql_error());
    mysql_select_db($this->vtable) or die("I am unable to select the database. " . mysql_error());

    return $this->vbuildDB();
}
```

I have called mysql_connect() to connect to the database. After that, I used mysql_select_db() to ensure that I save the data in the right spot. Both of these functions should be accompanied by the die() command. This ensures that if the function fails, the execution of the script stops, and the programmer sees a message to decide in which direction he should move now.

The connect() function will help you make a connection with the database and points you in the right direction. After that it runs buildDB() function. This function will run every time a user loads the page. Therefore, we ought to make sure that we are don't overwrite the database with every function call. When you have created the database, you have to fill it in with the content.

```
public function dis_admin() {
    return <<<ADMIN_FORM
    <form action="{$_SERVER['PHP_SELF']}" method="post">
        <label for="this is the title">Title:</label>
        <input name="this is the title" id="title" type="text" maxlength="200" />
        <label for="bodytext">Body Text:</label>
        <textarea name="bodytext" id="bodytext"></textarea>
```

```
        <input type="submit" value="Please create An
Entry!" />
    </form>

ADMIN_FORM;
}
```

This is a simple function. When you call it, it will simply return the HTML markup for the creation of the form. You will notice that in the *action* attribute of the *form* element, the variable $_SERVER['PHP_SELF'].

There is another method known as writeit() that will allow you to save the input information.

```
public function vwrite($p) {
    if ( $p['vtitle'] )
       $vtitle =
mysql_real_escape_string($p['vtitle']);
    if ( $p['vbodytext'])
       $vbodytext =
mysql_real_escape_string($p['vbodytext']);
    if ( $vtitle && $vbodytext ) {
       $vcreated = time();
       $sql = "You are required to INSERT the testDB
VALUES('$vtitle','$vbodytext','$vcreated')";
       return mysql_query($sql);
    } else {
       return false;
    }
}
```

Through the function call, you are passing a variable. The variable $p will hold the information sent from the form with the help of the post method. Once you get into the function, you may start with the help of a conditional statement.

Now that you have put information into the database, you may move on to carving out a way to get that information back and display it. For the purpose, you can use the display_public() function. This is perhaps the most complex of the methods. You really need to figure it out.

```php
public function dis_public() {
    $vq = "SELECT * FROM testDB";
    $vr = mysql_query($vq);

    if ( $vr !== false && mysql_num_rows($vr) > 0 )
{
        while ( $va = mysql_fetch_assoc($vr) ) {
           $vtitle = stripslashes($va['vtitle']);
           $vbodytext = stripslashes($va['vbodytext']);

           $entry_display .= <<<ENTRY_DISPLAY

        <h2>$vtitle</h2>
        <p>
          $vbodytext
        </p>

ENTRY_DISPLAY;
        }
     } else {
        $entry_display = <<<ENTRY_DISPLAY

        <h2>Here we are building a PHP app</h2>
        <p>
          There are no entries on the page.
          Would you like to come back soon, or just
click on the
          link below for the addition of a unique entry!
        </p>

ENTRY_DISPLAY;
     }
```

```
    $entry_display .= <<<ADMIN_OPTION

    <p class="admin_link">
      <a
href="{$_SERVER['PHP_SELF']}?admin=1">Please add a
fresh Entry here</a>
    </p>

ADMIN_OPTION;

    return $entry_display;
}
```

You can see how PHP and MySQL are interacting with each other. I asked the database a query to which it replied with a result. The result is not very handy until you succeed in decoding it by using a streak of methods that would fetch and organize the raw information, contained inside a usable form, otherwise known as an array.

The query is set up with the $vq variable. In MySQL, the asterisk (*) operator means everything. Hence, the query requests the database to select almost everything from the entries in the testDB. The entries will be displayed in reverse chronological order. As the query has been defined, we can now send it to the database by using the function mysql_query(). The result will be stored in the variable $vr. The conditional statement "IF mysql_query() in the script runs after that. If the variable $vr contains entries from the database, you will have to fetch the data. The information will be displayed in the form of an array, which is generally organized similarly to the table itself. The function mysql_fetch_assoc() will analyze the resource and break it down into associative array. The function will fetch one entry at a time. If you want to retrieve all the entries, you can use a while loop just like I have inserted in the code. The data contains slashed that are added after we save the information to the database. That's why you see stripslashes() in the code. There is a link to the bottom of the web app that allows users to add a fresh entry to the database when they visit the website.

You will have to create a new file and save your class in it. Name it displayclass.pgp. Save it in the same folder where you have saved classCMS.php.

```html
<html lang="en">
  <head>
    <title>classCMS</title>
  </head>

  <body>
<?php
    include_once('_class/classCMS.php');
    $obj = new classCMS();
    $obj->vhost = 'database.host.net';
    $obj->vusername = 'DB1234567';
    $obj->vpassword = 'DBpassword';
    $obj->vtable = 'DB1234567';
    $obj->vconnect();

    if ( $_POST )
      $obj->vwrite($_POST);

    echo ( $_GET['admin'] == 1 ) ? $obj->dis_admin() : $obj->dis_public();

?>
  </body>

</html>
```

While building this kind of application in which you have to handle user input, the foremost thing is to keep in mind that you should not trust anyone, especially the people who are using your website. People are in the habit of doing some unexpected stuff, whether on purpose or by accident, which means that they might hit upon bugs or other vulnerabilities in the website and exploit them for their personal benefit.

Common Errors

Programmers tend to make a lot of errors during the scriptwriting phase. Here is a rundown of the most common and fatal errors that programmers make when they build an application with PHP.

Global Variables

In some cases, programmers fail to initialize global variables in the right way. You may prevent the mistake by setting up register_globals directive to off. The users, whose register_globals are on might be abuse your website application. Customers might gain admin-level access to the system by running arbitrary codes on the website.

Chapter Nine

Relevance of PHP in Modern App Development

PHP is considered one of the highly popular programming languages across the world. Most top websites use it, thanks to the immense popularity of Content Management Systems like Drupal and WordPress. PHP has been in demand for developing a web application with the help of popular frameworks like Laravel and Sympfony. JavaScript-based Node.js challenged the existence of PHP. However, it couldn't dislodge it from the imperial position PHP has taken for a while. PHP is still being used by a big number of programmers.

PHP, even though it is one of the most object-oriented and efficient languages, is overlooked more often as an option to develop innovative and modern applications. The most common consensus among the developers and decision-makers is that it is highly popular among builders of CMS software apps that many websites use. It tends to excel in general programming projects like CMSes based eCommerce stores and web portals.

PHP remains at the heart of some of the highly popular and the most successful technology companies across the world, such as Blablacar, Facebook, and Slack. Slack is quite popular among businesses that have to manage a remote team of hundreds of employees. More businesses are opting to use PHP for building modern apps for their startups. PHP is getting better with each passing day, and it offers plenty of advantages for businesses and developers. Despite the stereotypes, it can work with WebSocket; however, it has its limitations.

You can opt for PHP if you have got a business that you wish to bring into the market as quickly as possible. The pace at which you launch your idea matters much when you are competing with a big number of businesses. To stay ahead of the competition, it is a good idea to be quick. A quick start will help you find unique business models that you might not have considered previously. If the business idea demands that you create a web application, PHP can be a perfect choice. You can use popular PHP framework Laravel and Symfony to create web applications in a really fast manner.

You can gauge the popularity of PHP from the fact that about 81% of the websites use PHP as a scripting language on the server-side. The rising popularity of PHP in modern app development is because of certain proven benefits.

Built-in Features

Unlike many other programming languages, PHP was initially designed for web application development. Therefore, the designers, from the very start, crammed it with special built-in features that were required to build different types of websites and web applications. You can use the built-in features such as functions and classes in PHP to perform a variety of web development operations and tasks. When you are building a program, you can call the classes and functions at any point in the code to perform specific tasks. This makes PHP easy and fun for building applications.

PHP supports a wide range of operating systems such as Mac OSX, Windows, and UNIX. The web applications that are written in PHP run on all major platforms. You also have the option of deploying PHP on IIS, Netscape, Apache, Personal Web server, and iPlanet server. Hence you can build PHP websites and applications without worrying about its hosting options and deployment.

Flexibility

PHP is a highly flexible language designed based on popular programming languages such as C++ and C.

You can easily read the script, understand it, and use the syntax of this server-side programming language without putting any kind of extra effort and time. You also have the option to write and use PHP code in many ways. Either you can embed it in the HTML code just like we did in all the codes in the book, or you can combine the code with web frameworks. You also can execute it by using a command-line interface.

Popular Databases

Most of the web applications nowadays consider accessing and delivering a big amount of data efficiently and quickly. Big business always wants to use high-level databases in the backend environment. PHP supports a bunch of widely used databases such as SQLite, MySQL, and Frontbase, including others. This is how you can cater to the needs of different business clients.

If we analyze PHP, we can realize the fact that, by using it, we can slash the coding time by a big margin by using a big number of open source libraries and frameworks. All depending on the requirements of the projects at hand, you can choose from different PHP frameworks such as CodeIgniter, CakePHP, and many others. These frameworks make coding simple and fast. You don't have to write lengthy scripts and complex codes by using common PHP libraries such as Requests, Mink, Ratchet, and Faker. PHP is distributed under an open-source license; therefore, you are allowed to use all components without spending anything on the licensing fees.

Benefits of PHP

Hypertext Preprocessor or PHP development has revolutionized the way web development was done in the past. There are no second thoughts on the possibility that PHP software development had been the most agile and advanced system that had been deployed for the development of dynamic and precise websites. PHP can cater to the needs of big enterprises. The functionalities that might be integrated into the websites must be smooth.

It is, without a doubt, the most favorite aspect as to why builders like it to customize big websites for the clients. This happens because there are plenty of advantages of using PHP. The Laravel PHP internal development is growing because of a brilliant authentication system. By using this, it becomes clean to apply authentication.

Simple API

Laravel Hypertext Preprocessor offers a smooth platform for sending in-app emails to different people through a cloud-based or neighborhood service. It also offers support to push notifications through dynamic channels such as Slack. An internet application is perfectly secured while it moves with the help of a professional development incorporation.

Optimization

Many B2C web applications should not only be really easy to use, but it also is easier to be found by the customers. eCommerce stores on the internet survive only if they have top-notch Search Engine Optimization services in place. If you want your web application to rank higher online, you must stuff it up with the most relevant keyword to rank in the most popular search engines. During the development phase, you ought to take into consideration these facts. Search engine crawlers like a clean HTML because it is easier to read. Creating clean code is one of the reasons PHP was created in the first place. Take the example of Wikipedia that pulls in tons of traffic each day. It is built with PHP language. Some experts say to the extent that each text-rich website that draws mind-boggling traffic is written in PHP.

App Stability

PHP has been faring well for the past two decades, and it has turned out to be a stable solution. Laravel and Symfony are being used for modern app development for several years. They have matured over time and got rid of most of the flaws that once plagued this language. Still, these frameworks are being constantly improved as the technological trends are changing, and the expectations of the developers are rising higher.

Maintenance

Unlike the other programming languages, PHP puts little to no emphasis on the readability and maintainability of the code. PHP frameworks tend to simplify the development of applications and maintenance by supporting a model-view-controller (MVC) architecture. Developers can take advantage of the architecture to break down PHP into views, models, and controllers. They can use this feature to separate business and interface logic layers. PHP also offers you to automate some common tasks in addition to writing the code for you.

Chapter Ten

Tips on PHP App Development

PHP has significantly improved itself over the past years in terms of speed and performance. It has become insanely speedy. There is type hinting for writing methods and return types, polishing the language, and making it more consistent. There are a bunch of helper methods to achieve more while at the same time writing less. If you have made up your mind to use PHP from now on for building websites and apps, you should migrate to PHP 7.

PHP is so popular that some big companies have chosen it to build their websites and apps such as Tumblr, Wikipedia, Facebook, TED, and National Geographic. Yes, Facebook runs on PHP. Developers love this language because it has such nice documentation. The community is massive in size, which means that you can have support all the time if some issues pop up along the way. PHP is highly reliable, mature, and stable. The PHP staff stay careful in throwing new functionalities that would break the old one. Also, they have a professional roadmap for the releases.

Most of the fame that is accredited to PHP is because of the PHP frameworks. There are two big players in the field that remain in a neck-on-neck competition all the time among developers. Both are really great and can make things fast for you. However, Laravel is considered more popular.

Laravel

This framework is created by Raylor Otwell and is defined as the best for Web Artisans. It has been around the corner since 2011. The best thing about Laravel is that it has a brilliantly easy curve. If you happen to be a traditional PHP developer, you will find it smooth to use. You can integrate it with queuing, Laravel mix, and caching as well. Its major characteristics include user management, login, user registration, notifications, and authentication system. These characteristics allow you to pace up your moves while you are building your application. The collections helper allows you to bring your data into an elegant form.

PHP Tips

Server-side languages were generally made to be highly complicated so that websites are the least vulnerable to malicious attacks. However, PHP has revolutionized the field by simplifying the server-side coding. Due to its open-source nature, PHP has been able to create a growing community of web developers who shaped it into the form it is now in today. The list of functions due to the brainstorming of those developers is endless, and the frameworks that can streamline your coding process have no end in sight.

Error Reporting Feature

The first on the line is the error reporting feature of PHP. Before you start working on a new project in PHP, you should turn on the error reporting feature of PHP. Even professional developers tend to swear by it. So, what will happen next? Throughout the production mode, you will get to see a bunch of helpful error messages instead of seeing a blank screen each time when a problem happens. It will help you cope with the errors as you scan the code. Overall, it will make the process of coding efficient and fast.

Include the following feature at the start of the script, and the error reporting feature will be automatically turned on. This will save you the pain of scanning thousands of lines of codes on your way to detect an error.

```
display_errors = on
```

Code Sketching

As with all the programs that you build with PHP, the end goal is the creation of a usable interface for the code. Before you take a dive into the development of a web application, you should make a sketch of your code and the data structure. You may need to have a clear idea of how you will desire to see your interface before you make a head start.

Stay Updated

PHP is considered a widely-used programming language. It receives fresh updates each day to match user requirements in a fast and efficient manner. If you want to stay ahead in this fierce competition, you should make yourself familiar with the updates to learn about the top ways to create a website.

Vocabulary

As you read through the book, you came across with a multitude of terms like constants, functions, classes, and interfaces. These terms form the bulk of the PHP vocabulary. There are other terms like variables, comments, inheritance, methods, and properties. Learning these terms and understanding them are the keys to making your website application highly efficient and highly functional. If you master these terms, it will help you streamline your coding and make your program better than others. They help you accomplish a task in the best possible way, and they also add a bunch of unique features to the app you are building. You can check out a manual on the official PHP website, php.net, to expand your vocabulary and to have an in-depth understanding of this programming language. The manual covers everything from the basic syntax to the supporter protocols. A good vocabulary is also the key to highly advanced skills.

OOP

If you have not yet stepped into the world of object-oriented programming, you have put yourself at a disadvantage. You will eventually fall behind fast. OOP, as you have studied in-depth in the past sections of the book, revolves around classes or objects, which keeps different things tied together. They eliminate the need for the elimination of code and help you perform basic tasks simple. Objects are classes that integrate into themselves different functions and allow developers to use them over and over again during the developing phase. This allows you to reuse the code when you ought to do something.

Comments

Many novice developers believe that they should not waste time on making commentaries. However, the truth is that it is a habit that you should pick up as early as possible in your life. As a developer, you should be as attentive as you are when you are writing the code. Each comment works as a reference for you to know what you have written and what you have written. These comments tend to explain which direction your program or application is going to take.

However, adding comments to your code doesn't mean that you clutter it with comments. Just make a few short notes to make the code readable so that when you come back to the start after finishing the code, you don't have to guess at what you have written. Another method is documenting the code for complicated sections in the file so that you can decipher some highly complex details. You must not forget to change the comments when you are changing the code, or it will leave you wondering what it's all about.

PHP Frameworks

PHP frameworks are designed to help developers. If you happen to be an ideal coder, you will need to have weeks or months before you can create a web application from scratch. Most of the time will be consumed on the production of repetitive code, which is boring. If you are willing to invest time and effort, you should go for it. Otherwise, use a framework such as Laravel, which I have already explained in this book.

As a web developer, you look forward to creating high-quality products to make big money and win good graces of your clients. However, writing everything from scratch is the worst strategy in the world of coding. PHP frameworks offer a viable solution to these problems. A framework also ensures a connection between your database and application.

Conclusion

Now that you have made it to the end of the book, I hope you have learned a lot about the basics of PHP scripting language. I have given you practical codes, instructions, and in-depth explanations in the book so that you can use them to understand the scripts, and you can edit them to create unique scripts. If you get to apply the lessons that you have studied in the book, you will become a skilled user in a short period.

Apart from brute force attacks that aim at guessing your password by using the login screen, bots that work day and night to exploit the vulnerabilities in the website's PHP code are considered the most common form of attacks that target the vulnerabilities in your websites. You have to keep into consideration the vulnerabilities in PHP coding so that you can remove them and make your PHP code stronger.

Remote Code Execution is the attack that occurs when a hacker uploads malicious code to a website and also executes it right away. If there is a bug in PHP, it will accept malicious input by a user and reads it as a PHP code. This allows the hacker to instruct the website to create a new file that contains the code which will grant the malicious hacker complete access to the website. When the hacker sends the code to the web application, and it is executed well in time, it will grant access to the hacker to your website. In this way, they can successfully exploit an RCE vulnerability.

SQL Injection is another vulnerability that a hacker can exploit to attack your web application. Through a SQL Injection, a hacker can dispatch malicious instructions to the web applications' database. The web app database executes the instructions due to a vulnerability in the code and lets the hacker in. This kind of attack generally happens when a web developer does not install a sanitization barrier for the input from the users. This allows a malicious user to fill in the web app with malicious code. SQL Injection will allow a hacker to access the website data. Hackers can create new data in the database that may contain links to spam websites. The attacker may use SQL Injection to create an administrator account and use it to gain full control of your website application. The best way to stay safe from this kind of vulnerability is to put in place a barrier for the sanitization of input from the users. The input should be verified first and then permitted to enter the database of the website.

Cross-Site Scripting (XSS) can happen when a malicious hacker finds a way to load malicious code on the website and execute it as well. This malicious code can grant administrative access to the malicious hacker. A stored XSS happens when a malicious hacker gets the website to store malicious code that is later on served up within the browser of another user and executed accordingly. A practical example is when the hacker posts a comment containing malicious code on a WordPress website. Reflected XSS happens when an attacker creates a link that contains malicious code and loads the link to the browser. The website reads it as website content. The code executes in the user's browser after that and may let the hacker steal cookies or perform malicious tasks.

These are some of the web application vulnerabilities that you should consider after you learn PHP. This book is the complete package for learning the ins and outs of PHP. I have explained the main topics in detail so that you get to know how a website application works. The two major parts of a website are explained in detail. You can leverage on this practical information and enhance your knowledge further in the world of web applications.

Resources

1. https://css-tricks.com/php-for-beginners-building-your-first-simple-cms/
2. http://www.allaboutweb.biz/advantages-of-php-in-web-application-development/
3. https://tsh.io/blog/when-is-php-used-in-modern-app-development/
4. https://khmerbamboo.files.wordpress.com/2014/09/php-mysql-javascript-html5-all-in-one-for-dummies.pdf
5. https://www.thirdstage-marketing.com/10-php-tips-tricks-every-web-developer-know/
6. https://www.w3schools.com/php/php_if_else.asp
7. https://www.w3schools.com/php/php_looping.asp
8. https://www.w3schools.com/php/php_functions.asp
9. https://www.w3schools.com/php/php_oop_classes_objects.asp
10. https://www.w3schools.com/php/php_oop_inheritance.asp
11. https://www.w3schools.com/php/php_oop_destructor.asp
12. https://www.w3schools.com/php/php_oop_constructor.asp
13. https://www.w3schools.com/sql/sql_select.asp
14. https://www.w3schools.com/sql/sql_distinct.asp
15. https://www.w3schools.com/sql/sql_where.asp
16. https://www.w3schools.com/sql/sql_and_or.asp
17. https://www.w3schools.com/sql/sql_orderby.asp
18. https://www.w3schools.com/sql/sql_update.asp
19. https://www.w3schools.com/sql/sql_delete.asp

Made in the USA
Columbia, SC
25 May 2024